GAIL SELFRIDGE'S

SWEATER DESIGN WORKBOOK

25.50

I0904564

interweave

Gail Selfridge's

Sweater Design Workbook

Interweave Press

©1991, Gail Selfridge
All rights reserved.

 INTERWEAVE PRESS, INC.
201 East Fourth Street
Loveland, Colorado 80537

COVER: SIGNORELLA GRAPHIC ARTS

First printing: 391:7.5M:OB/CL

ISBN: 0-934026-65-3

CIP Data:
  Selfridge, Gail.
    [Sweater design workbook]
    Gail Selfridge's sweater design workbook.
      p.   cm.
    Includes bibliographical references.
    ISBN 0-934026-65-3 : $14.95
     1. Knitting--Patterns.   2. Sweaters.   I. Title.   II. Title:
  Sweater design workbook.
  TT825.S45   1991
  746.9'2--dc20   90-56185
                                        CIP

Table of Contents

Preface

Everything you need to design and knit successful one-of-a-kind sweaters is right here in this book:

—One simple, fool-proof, versatile sweater pattern that can be sized and styled to suit everyone from babies to extra-large adults.

—A set of knitters' graph papers in 20 different gauges.

If you know how to knit and purl, increase and decrease, and cast on and bind off, you can use the Basic Sweater pattern to design for everyone in the family, using any weight of yarn and the needles of your choice. You can use it to knit by hand or by machine. The simple modular pattern can be varied for crew, V-, or turtle necks, inset, saddle, or dropped shoulders, slipovers or cardigans.

You can use the Gauged Graph Paper, especially proportioned to match the stitches and rows per inch of your gauge swatch, to chart out the design of your choice, just as it will appear when knitted into your sweater. You can also use the Graph Paper to guide you through shape modifications of the Basic Sweater and even to create your own sweater styles. This versatile Graph Paper, plus the handy Worksheet, is all the pattern you'll ever need.

The more we've used this pattern, the more we've appreciated its versatility. We hope you'll find it useful, too.

Ann Budd and Linda Ligon, editors

Introduction

I was first introduced to knitting through a women's organization which made knitted mittens to sell at a church bazaar. Anyone who wanted to participate was welcome, including those who didn't know how to knit, as an instructor had been engaged to teach the basic techniques. What an opportunity. I had always wanted to learn how to knit, but wasn't quite able to accomplish it from books. I went to the lessons and was absolutely fascinated with the process.

At the time, I was employed as a scientific illustrator of plant and animal specimens—exacting work that required meticulous attention to detail. Knitting became an enjoyable diversion. I eagerly looked forward to working on mittens at the end of each day. But when I finally finished the first pair, I was quite surprised and disappointed. The mittens were supposed to fit children, but they were big enough for adults. The basic instruction had not impressed upon me the meaning and the necessity of "gauge". However, I had learned the fundamentals of the process, and armed with these, I was able to continue working to improve my technique. Subsequent mittens were much better, and soon I wanted to tackle a larger project. A sweater was the next item on the agenda.

After purchasing a pattern, needles, and yarn, I went home to begin work on my sweater. About halfway into the project I started to experience difficulties. Some things just didn't look right, but I was so inexperienced that I didn't know either what was wrong or what to do about it. I lived a long way from my yarn dealer, so instead of just going there and asking questions, I chose to deal with it myself. Being a visual thinker, I decided what I needed was a diagram. Though I was experienced at developing drawings and illustrations, it was no easy task to draw a diagram of the parts and convert it to a working pattern of stitches and rows—all the instructions were written in "knitting-ese".

I've planned and executed many sweaters since that time, but the seeds of the Gail Selfridge Basic Sweater Pattern were sown in that first sweater project, and the pattern that you see today evolved from those humble beginnings. Throughout the developmental process, the use of diagrams to establish parameters for each of the parts has always been the distinguishing feature of my knitted designs. Unlike traditional designers who first sketch an entire garment as one unit and then try to figure out how it could possibly be knitted, I have always started by drawing flat diagrams of the parts (front, back, sleeves) and then modifying those shapes with knitting techniques (often simple increases and/or decreases) to produce style changes.

Because my days were spent drawing, it was only a matter of time until my drawings were converted into knitting motifs. The first time I tried to do this I used squared graph paper to plot a motif. I remember being quite surprised that the knitted image didn't match the drawing. It was then that I realized that of course it wouldn't match—there were more knitted divisions vertically (rows) than there were horizontally (stitches). So I took some plain paper and ruled graph paper that exactly matched the stitch and row proportions of my knitted sample. Being naive about knitting pedagogy, I assumed that was what everyone did, and each time I encountered a new gauge I ruled a new paper.

Charting motifs was challenging, and producing a good motif took a lot of time. Because I wanted to extend the usefulness of each motif, I drew diagrams for a group of garments and home items (toys, afghans, and such) and divided them into 2-, 4-, 6-, and 8-inch squares. I then charted motifs to fit those square units. The process resembled that used by children to create buildings from modular blocks, and I called it "Patchwork Knitting".

Patchwork Knitting was "discovered" by Theresa Capuana of *Woman's Day* magazine, and my idea was used as the basis for a group of garments and home items in that magazine. The article led to my first book, *Patchwork Knitting*. In addition to many projects and motifs, I also devised for that book a group of modular yokes for sweaters. These yokes were originally intended simply to accommodate motifs based upon 4-, 6-, and 8-inch square units; however, during the production of the prototypes I discovered a fringe benefit: these modular yokes were great sizing devices. And not only could the yokes be used to size garments, but the resulting sweater pattern appeared to have endless possibilities for producing style modifications. The Gail Selfridge Basic Sweater pattern was born.

Since that time my pattern has been, like all children, growing by venturing into the bigger world. Over the years I have used it to create many designs for yarn companies, needlework publications, and books. I have also used it to create garments for myself and members of my family. In addition, I have used the pattern to teach other knitters how to be creative in their knitting. This is where my pattern and method of working have proven most satisfying.

In teaching adults, I found that many of them believed design was beyond their capabilities. After analyzing this situation, I attributed this belief not to a lack of ideas or creativity, but rather to the fact that design is often intricately fused with sizing. It would follow that by using a systematic method for dealing with sizing the knitter would then be free to concentrate on design elements. A sweater could become a blank canvas for creative expression.

With the publication of this book, my pattern officially becomes an adult. Originally titled and sold by me as *Design Kit*, the work sounded academic and read much like an algebra text. It was a child that perhaps only a mother could love. Linda Ligon and Ann Budd have worked diligently to create a "user-friendly" edition in an attempt to reach a great many more knitters with this unique approach to knitting. It is my sincere desire that this method of knitting prove as useful and creatively satisfying to each of you as it has to me.

The Basic Sweater

Every sweater is essentially a set of three tubes—one large tube for the body and two smaller tubes for the arms. The most difficult part of developing sweater patterns that are simple and yet fit well is fitting the arms to the body. Shaped armholes and sleeve caps often result in a sweater that's too tight where the arms join to the body; drop-shoulder sweaters, on the other hand, are often baggy and unbecoming. The Basic Sweater in this book solves this problem with a simple design concept, the modular yoke. This yoke is the key to sizing the sweater; it allows for neat and simple set-in square sleeves, and it provides a large rectangular area that can easily be patterned with color motifs.

The following step-by-step instructions for the Basic Sweater apply to all sweater sizes. For first sweater projects, I recommend using sport weight yarn (for machine knitting) or worsted (for hand knitting) in a light color (so you can see what you're doing more easily).

Step One: Constructing gauge swatches

It's easy to underestimate the importance of gauge. Even experienced knitters can forget that just a fraction of a stitch per inch, when multiplied around the circumference of a sweater, can make several inches' difference in size. So it's no wonder that beginning knitters sometimes are so eager to begin that they omit the gauge swatch as a first step. Whether you are following an existing pattern or creating a new design, making a gauge swatch should always be your first step.

The gauge is the number of stitches per inch and the number of rows per inch of knitted fabric. Taking the gauge means counting *exactly* the number of stitches (and fractions of stitches), and the number of rows, for each inch of knitted fabric. If you are following a printed pattern, you must exactly match the gauge that it specifies in order to end up with a garment that's the right

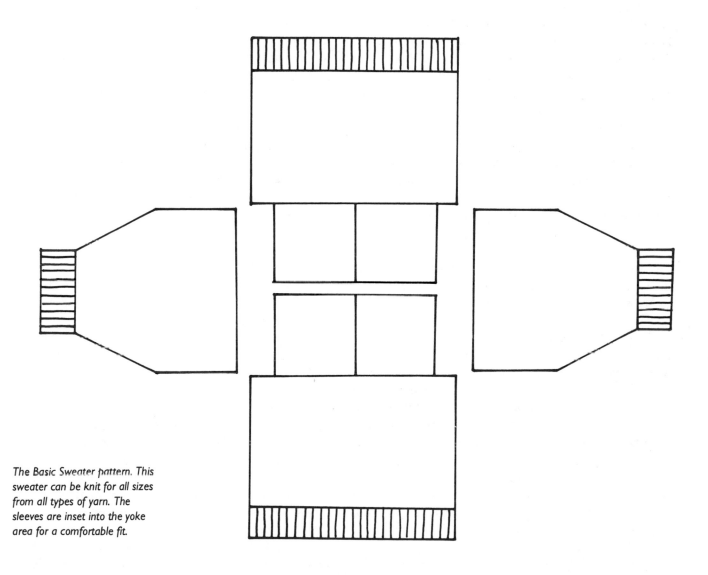

The Basic Sweater pattern. This sweater can be knit for all sizes from all types of yarn. The sleeves are inset into the yoke area for a comfortable fit.

The Basic Sweater

■

size. If you are creating a new pattern, you'll need to know how many stitches and rows there are per inch of knitted fabric in order to calculate working directions from your own measurements.

To determine the gauge of a given yarn, you must first knit a sample swatch of fabric using the same yarn and stitch pattern that you will be using in the proposed project. In hand knitting, these samples are called gauge swatches; in machine knitting (and among British hand knitters), they are usually referred to as tension swatches.

For both hand and machine knitting, making these swatches gives you an opportunity to experiment with the yarn and achieve the desired look and feel and a chance to see how the knitted fabric will launder. It makes no difference whether you are working from a commercial pattern or from one of your own designs, constructing a sample swatch, or as often happens, a series of sample swatches, is always your first step.

Hand knitting. Hand knitters often use commercial yarns for which recommended needle sizes and gauges are given. To make a gauge swatch for such a yarn, cast on at least 20 stitches using the specified yarn and needle size. Gauge swatches are made in stockinette stitch (knit one row, purl one row) unless the pattern specifies another stitch. Work until the piece measures 4 inches long, then bind off. This should give you a piece approximately 3 to 4 inches by 4 inches. If your yarn is very irregular or very heavy, you'll be able to get a more accurate gauge count if you knit a larger swatch, perhaps as much as 10 inches square.

At this point, steam the swatch lightly just as you would a finished knitted item. Lay it on a flat surface. Center your gauge ruler and count horizontally to determine the number of stitches per inch and vertically for the number of rows per inch. For best accuracy, measure across 2 inches and divide the resulting number

by 2 to get the number of stitches or rows in one inch to see if, indeed, it matches the gauge recommended by the manufacturer. Do not round off when measuring! If, for example, you get 6½ stitches per inch, you should not round off to 6 or 7. Your gauge is 6½ stitches per inch, or 13 stitches per 2 inches. The same rules apply to measuring rows.

If your gauge doesn't match, you must adjust it before beginning to knit. Keep in mind that if you are off gauge by as little as a quarter of a stitch per inch in your gauge swatch, your sweater will quite likely be several inches too big or too small. The rules for adjusting the gauge are:

—If your gauge has fewer stitches per inch than required (loose tension), then you should knit another sample using the next size smaller needles.

—If your gauge has more stitches per inch than required (tight tension), then knit another sample using the next size larger needles.

Continue to do this until your gauge corresponds to the one specified.

If you are using a yarn that doesn't come labeled with a recommended gauge or needle size, you have two options. First, consult an interchangeable yarn chart (your yarn shop should have one). If the yarn is listed, it will be accompanied by a suggested gauge and needle size, and you can work from there. If the yarn is not listed on the interchangeable yarn chart (weaving yarns, imports, and handspun yarns, for example), you will have to rely upon your experience to guide you—pick a needle size that looks right and start knitting. The conventional rules of thumb are that sport weight yarns (1200–1800 yards per pound) usually use size 4 to 6 needles (US sizes), worsted yarns (1000–1200 yards per pound) usually use size 7 to 9, and bulky yarns (600–1000 yards per pound) usually use size 10 or 11 needles.

When using an unknown yarn, it is a good idea to knit several swatches using different needle sizes. Each one will have a slightly different feel. Some will be firmer, some softer, some drapier—you can choose the effect you want. As you finish each swatch, label it with the needle size for future reference. These sample swatches may be the only source of information available to you regarding the gauge of a particular yarn and the properties of the resulting knitted fabric.

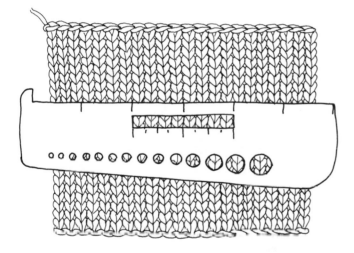

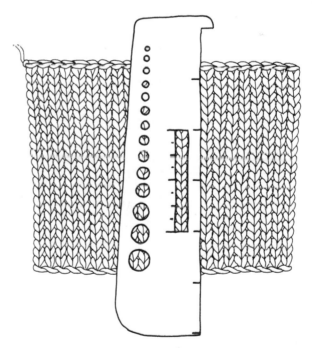

To measure the stitch gauge on a hand-knitted swatch, align the gauge ruler along a row of stitches, count the number of stitches within a 2-inch width, and divide by 2. To measure the row gauge, align the gauge ruler along a column of stitches, count the number of stitches within a 2-inch length, and divide by 2. In this example, there are 8 stitches and 12 rows per 2 inches. The gauge then, is 4 stitches and 6 rows per inch.

The Basic Sweater

■

Size 6 needles

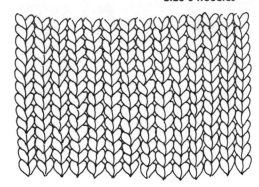

These three swatches were all knitted with the same yarn. However, the needle size varied from size 6 to size 10, resulting in three different gauges (5½ x 9, 5 x 8, and 5 x 7). The smaller the needle size, the tighter the gauge and the firmer the fabric. More subtle differences in gauge occur between consecutive needle sizes.

Size 8 needles

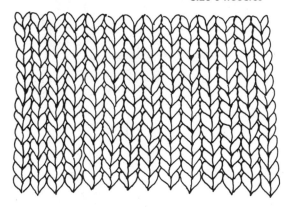

Size 10 needles

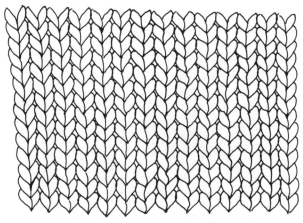

Machine knitting. Tension swatches are usually made on 100 stitches or, if your yarn is heavy and you are using every other needle, 50 stitches. Do not make your swatches too small. Samples that are too small stretch more easily and give the illusion of a fabric that is softer and more pliable than it would be in a larger piece.

Tension swatches can be made using either an open or closed cast-on. (I prefer to use a closed cast-on and to bind off the last row, thus producing an entirely closed sample.) Once you have decided on the number of stitches to use, cast them on and work for 100 to 150 rows (or just 50 for heavier yarns). There are no rules about the exact size of these samples, but when you have made a few, you'll develop a feel for approximately how big they should be. After working the desired number of rows, remove the swatch from the needle bed with a hand knitting needle and bind off by hand.

Usually you will make several gauge swatches with the same yarn using different tension settings and stitch sizes. As with hand knitting, it is a good habit to label each swatch with the tension setting and stitch size for future reference as soon as you remove it from the machine.

After removing the swatch from the needles, pull it gently into shape. Unlike hand-knitted samples that achieve their dimensions as the knitting progresses, machine knits need this gentle lengthwise pulling to establish their shape. This is an important step; if you skip it, your resulting gauge measurements will be inaccurate.

Steam the swatch lightly and lay it on a flat surface. Using a flexible measuring tape, measure the length and width of the sample. Divide the number of stitches by the width to establish the stitch gauge; divide the number of rows by the length to establish the row gauge. A calculator is useful for this procedure. Many calculators show several decimal places—round off to the nearest quarter stitch or row per inch. Use a gauge ruler as described for hand knits if you want to compare the gauge of a small isolated area against that of the large swatch.

Developing a series of swatches

Testing a variety of needle sizes to get a fabric that "looks and feels right" is an important part of the design process. If you are not accustomed to designing your own knits, this procedure may seem tedious and time consuming. But after the first few projects, it simply becomes part of the knitting process. Enthusiasm for making swatches results from experiencing the rewards.

To develop an appropriate knitted fabric from an unfamiliar yarn, start by knitting one sample. Remove it from the needles, label it, and record the following information: tension setting, stitch size, number of strands of yarn used, and needle positions for machine knits; needle size for hand knits. Make two additional samples, one by decreasing the stitch size (smaller needles) and/or increasing the tension to give a fabric that is heavier and stiffer than the original, and the other sample by increasing the stitch size (larger needles) and/or decreasing the tension to give a fabric that is softer and more supple than the original. Label these two samples as above.

If you plan to use several different colors or kinds of yarn within one project, knit them into the swatches in approximately the same proportions that they will appear in the finished piece. The essence of success with this technique lies in avoiding the feeling of being rushed or hurried to make only a single test piece and then plunging ahead. Take time to experiment with several swatches. The rewards of this effort will soon be evident in the feel, fit, and drape of your sweaters.

The Basic Sweater

■

Choosing the appropriate knitted fabric

Your project determines your choice of fabric. Once your sample swatches are finished, try to visualize how they would look and feel if used in your proposed project. For example, a sweater requires a soft, supple fabric; dolls or stuffed animals can be made from the same yarn as a sweater, but they require a much heavier and stiffer fabric. You would probably choose a softer fabric for a baby sweater than you would for a man's outdoor cardigan, and a drapier fabric for a dressy sweater than for a rugged one.

From your series of samples, pick the one that you believe best fits your project. (If none of your samples is quite right, go back to your machine or needles and try different stitch or needle sizes.) Once you have selected the most appropriate swatch and recorded the gauge, you'll have the information you need to convert the inches of your diagram or formula into a working pattern of stitches and rows.

The sample swatches that you didn't select can be unraveled and reused in the final project or, if you have enough yarn, save these samples for future reference. If you decide to use the same yarn again in a different project, you may have already knitted the right swatch— depending, of course, upon the nature of the additional project.

Keep in mind that the heart of creating beautiful, well-fitting knits lies in these sample swatches. Thus, the time and effort invested in your swatches will be richly rewarded with superior finished products.

Recording the gauge

After you have worked out your gauge information for a particular yarn, record it for future use. You may find it handy to store all of your yarn information on index cards in a file box. Because you may wish to use the same yarns for both hand and machine knitting projects, take care to identify the pertinent information about each project the yarn is used for.

On your cards include the gauge (that is, the number of stitches and the number of rows per inch), the size of the needle used or the tension setting and stitch size, the number of strands used, and the machine needle positions (that is, did you use every needle, every second needle, or every third needle?).

For future reference, you may also want to record the name of the yarn and its manufacturer, size or weight of the balls or skeins, and fiber content.

What a sample swatch tells you

In addition to telling you the gauge to which a particular yarn will knit, a sample swatch can also tell you the following things about the properties of the knitted fabric:

■ The appearance of the fabric.

Often knitted yarn undergoes surprising changes when it is transformed from skeins or cones into knitted fabric. Sample swatches tell you how the yarn both looks and feels once it has been knitted.

■ The success of color combinations.

Different colors of yarn that seem compatible in the unknitted state may be surprisingly unattractive when placed together in a piece of finished knitting. When devising a new color combination, knit a swatch using the colors as they will appear in the finished project to see if, indeed, the colors work well together.

■ How well the fabric will launder.

By laundering your sample, you can test its general laundering qualities and discover if it is color-fast and/or has any special problems. For example, 100% cotton may shrink, particularly if machine-dried. If your sample changes in any way during the laundering process, compute the gauge measurements from the laundered sample. (You will also want to include this information on your index cards.)

Record information about your yarns and gauge on index cards. This will eliminate the need to knit duplicate gauge swatches if the same yarn is to be used for a second, similar project.

The Basic Sweater

■

Step Two: Making your sweater pattern

The following instructions will help you to figure the measurements for a sweater that will fit well. Keep in mind that "moving space", or ease, can vary, and these are only suggested amounts. It is also possible to take measurements from an existing sweater, in which case you wouldn't need to add moving space (it's already included).

As you take your measurements, enter them on a copy of the Worksheet. (Note: Never write on the master Worksheet. Record the measurements on a photocopy of the master.)

Front and back width. Measure your chest and add moving space. A rule of thumb is to add 2 inches to adult sizes for a tailored fit (more for a "relaxed" look), 1 ½ inches for children, and 1 inches for infants. Divide the resulting figure by 2. This gives you the width, in inches, for both the front and back. Enter this figure on your Worksheet.

Now that you know the chest circumference, you can select the appropriate modular yoke pattern from the diagrams shown on pages 20–21. The layout diagrams on pages 22–24 are scaled to three modular yoke sizes. Choose the one that's appropriate for your sweater. If your sweater is to be larger than 40 inches in circumference, use a 10-inch or 12-inch yoke and follow the layout for the 8-inch-yoke sweater.

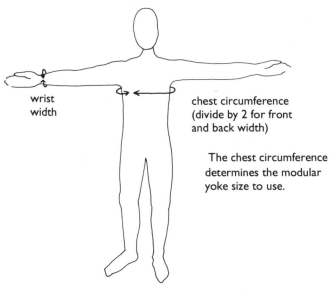

wrist width

chest circumference (divide by 2 for front and back width)

The chest circumference determines the modular yoke size to use.

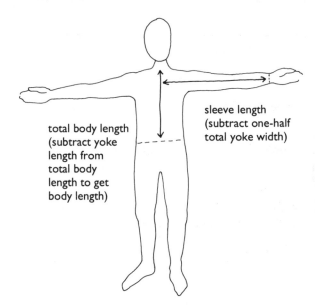

total body length (subtract yoke length from total body length to get body length)

sleeve length (subtract one-half total yoke width)

Take measurements as shown and record them on a photocopy of the Worksheet. Use your gauge information to convert inches of the pattern to numbers of stitches and number of rows. The Worksheet then becomes your working pattern. A master copy of this Worksheet is at the back of this book—make a new photocopy of the master for each project. It's a good idea to save your Worksheets for future reference after you've finished a project.

WORKSHEET: making a working pattern

Record your measurements on this worksheet. Then use you gauge information to convert inches of the pattern to numbers of stitches and numbers of rows.

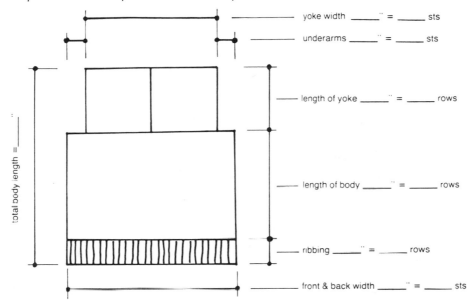

yoke width _____" = _____ sts

underarms _____" = _____ sts

length of yoke _____" = _____ rows

length of body _____" = _____ rows

ribbing _____" = _____ rows

front & back width _____" = _____ sts

total body length = _____

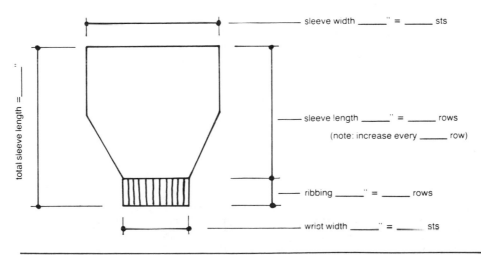

sleeve width _____" = _____ sts

sleeve length _____" = _____ rows

(note: increase every _____ row)

ribbing _____" = _____ rows

wrist width _____" = _____ sts

total sleeve length = _____

YARN & MACHINE NOTES:

hem notes (optional) _____" = _____ rows

The Basic Sweater

■

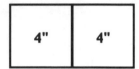

Infants and toddlers—the 4-inch base yoke
This is the yoke for the infant and toddler sweater. It is based on four 4-inch squares. This yoke is used to make sizes 16"–24".

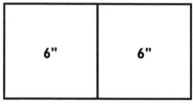

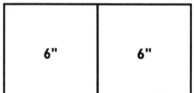

Children—the 6-inch base yoke
This is the yoke for the child's sweater. It is based on four 6-inch squares. This yoke is used to make sizes 24"–32".

Adults—the 8-inch base yoke
This is the yoke for the adult sweater. It is based on four 8-inch squares. This yoke is used to make sizes 32"–40".

10"	10"
10"	10"

Larger sizes

As you can see from the preceding yokes, larger sizes require correspondingly larger yoke bases.

Four 10-inch squares will give you a yoke for sizes 40"–48".

Four 12-inch squares will give you a yoke for sizes 48"–56".

These larger yoke sizes do not have corresponding sweater diagrams. Follow the diagram for the adult sweater, substituting a larger yoke base.

The modular yokes are scaled to chest measurements. For infant and toddler sizes, use a 4-inch base; for children, a 6-inch base; and for most adults, an 8-inch base. For larger sizes, use a 10- or 12-inch base. The Basic Sweater has both a front and back yoke, each made up of two base squares set side by side. The combined front and back yokes form a larger square, twice the size of the base square. In its simplest version, the yokes of the Basic Sweater butt-join at the shoulder, with a slit left unjoined for the neck opening.

The Basic Sweater

■

Body length. Measure from the top of the shoulder to the point at which you want the bottom edge of the sweater, including the ribbing. This is the total body length. Allow for some blousing in length if you like an easy fit. The total body length is the sum of the yoke length and the body length. The yoke lengths are indicated on the layout diagrams. Subtract the length of the yoke (shoulder to underarm) from the total body length. The resulting figure is the length of the body front and back. Enter the body length and the yoke length on your Worksheet.

Underarms. Subtract the width of the yoke (shoulder to shoulder) from the width of the front.

Divide the resulting number by 2. This gives you the number of inches to bind off for each underarm. Record this on your Worksheet.

Sleeve length. Measure from wrist to center back, adding a little ease if you wish. Subtract one half of the total yoke width. The resulting figure is the arm length or total length of the sleeve. Enter it on your Worksheet.

Wrist width. Measure around your wrist. Add moving space (adults 2 inches, children 1 ½ inches, infants 1 inch). Enter the resulting figure on the Worksheet.

Layout Diagram for Infants and Toddlers
   Use the 4-inch base yoke for infants and toddlers, size 16" to 24" chest. According to statistics, the average chest circumference of a newborn infant is 13.1". The average chest circumference of a 6-month baby is 17.2". If you want the sweater to fit baby for more than a couple of weeks, I recommend a minimum front and back width of 16".

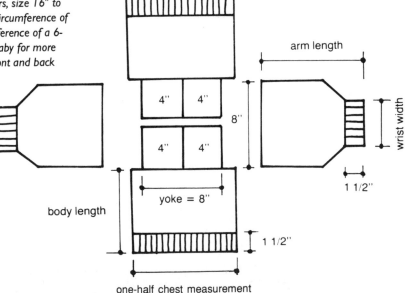

Sleeve width. The total sleeve width is the same as the combined length of both front and back yokes. Consult the appropriate layout diagram to determine this measurement. Then enter this figure on your Worksheet.

Finishing edges. The bottom edges of the sweater body and sleeves can have either a ribbed band or a hem.

Hem—Determine the length of the desired hem (suggested amounts: adults 3 inches, children 2 inches, infants 1½ inches). Make a notation on your Worksheet to add the required inches for the turned-under part of the hem.

Ribbed band—Determine the length of ribbing you wish to use (suggested amounts: adults 3 inches, children 2 inches, infants 1½ inches). Make a notation on your Worksheet showing the number of inches of the body that are devoted to the ribbed band.

Note: When making ribbing, either by hand or by machine, I like to use a K1, P1 stitch. This requires an even number of stitches, that is, a number divisible by 2. If your gauge gives you an uneven number of stitches, then subtract one stitch. For snug-fitting ribbing, some knitters use 10% or so fewer stitches for the ribbings and then increase to the appropriate number of stitches on the last row of ribbing.

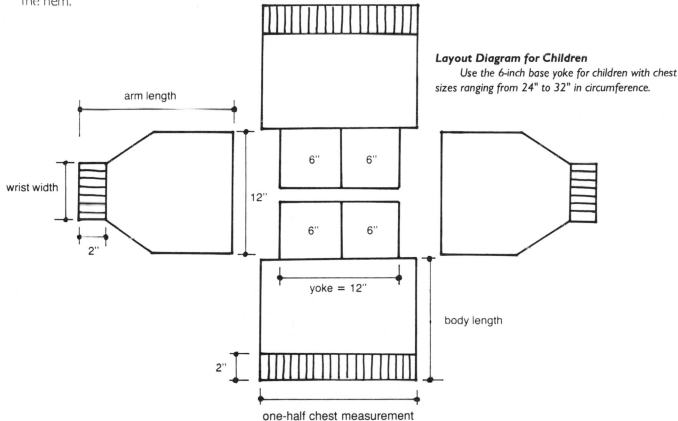

Layout Diagram for Children
Use the 6-inch base yoke for children with chest sizes ranging from 24" to 32" in circumference.

The Basic Sweater

■

Layout Diagram for Adults

Use the 8-inch base yoke for adults with chest circumferences ranging from 32" to 40". By substituting larger yokes, this diagram can also be used to compute sizes 40" to 56".

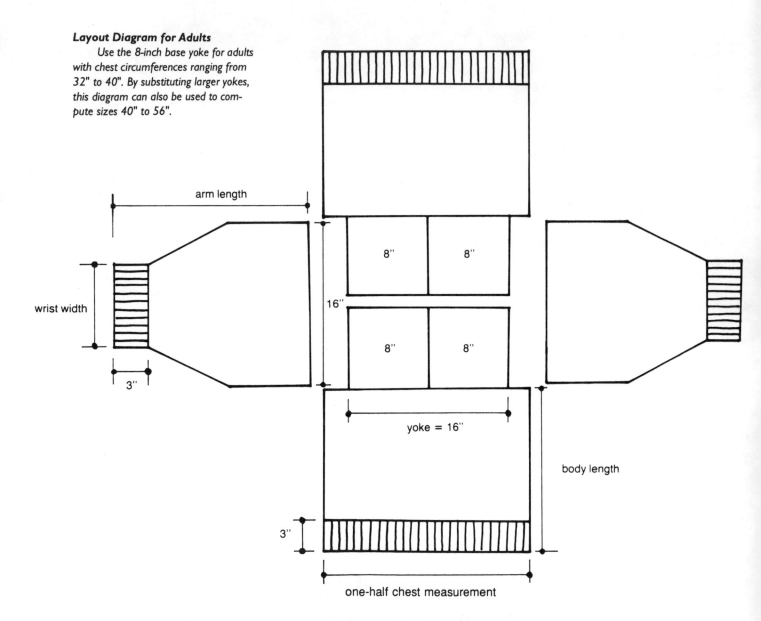

arm length

wrist width

3"

8"   8"

16"

8"   8"

yoke = 16"

body length

3"

one-half chest measurement

Converting measurements to stitches and rows

Once you have calculated your measurements and recorded them on the Worksheet, use the figures of your stockinette gauge to convert the inches of the diagram into a working pattern of stitches and rows.

To convert the number of inches to stitches, multiply the number of inches by your gauge. For example, if your body width is 20 inches and your gauge is 6 stitches per inch, you would need:

(20 inches) × (6 stitches per inch) = 120 stitches.

The number of rows are calculated in the same manner. If you need a piece to be 16 inches long and have a gauge of 8 rows per inch, you would need:

(16 inches) × (8 rows per inch) = 128 rows.

In some cases, your gauge will be such that your calculations will not result in a whole number of stitches per inch. When this is the case, a simple rule of thumb is to round to the nearest even number. For example, if your body width is 19 inches and your gauge is 6.5 stitches per inch, you would calculate:

(19 inches) × (6.5 stitches per inch) = 123.5 stitches,
which you would round to 124.

If your Worksheet calculations specify a fraction of a row, round up to the next whole row. For example, if your gauge is 7 rows per inch and your piece needs to be 17.5 inches long, you would calculate:

(17.5 inches) × (7 rows per inch) = 122.5 rows,
which you would round up to 123 rows.

Now you have a working pattern and are ready to knit your garment following the numbers on the Worksheet.

Step Three: Getting down to knitting

Hand knitting

Bottom edges of body and sleeves. Choose either a hemmed or ribbed bottom.

Hem—With needles two sizes smaller than those used to get the gauge, cast on the required number of stitches. (The smaller needles will prevent that bulky look that knitted hems often have.) Work the inches of the hem in stockinette. Make a turning ridge by having the knit side toward you and doing one row of purl (that is, purl three consecutive rows at the turning row).

Ribbing—Make a ribbed band by casting on the required number of stitches using needles two sizes smaller than those used to get gauge. Work in K1, P1 ribbing for the required number of inches for the band.

Body front and back. After knitting the hem or ribbing, work the next row and all subsequent rows with the same size needles used to get the correct gauge. Work in stockinette stitch for the appropriate number of rows to the underarms. Bind off the appropriate number of underarm stitches at the beginning of the next two rows. The remaining stitches constitute the yoke. Work the yoke for the required length and bind off.

Sleeves. If using a hem, use needles two sizes smaller than the gauge needle to knit the turned-under part of the hem. Change to larger needles after the turning row. Work until the sleeve length corresponds to the length of the hem before beginning your increases.

If using ribbing, change to larger needles and start increases on the first row after the ribbed band is completed.

The Basic Sweater
■

Increases—Increases should be placed one (or two) stitches in from each edge. Increase on knit rows in the following manner: Knit one stitch; in the next stitch knit and increase; work across row to the last three stitches; knit and increase in the next stitch; knit the remaining two stitches.

Increase rows should be spaced about one inch apart. If, for example, your gauge has 8 rows per inch, you would increase one stitch at each side of the sleeve every 8th row. You may find it's easier to remember when to increase if you always work the increases on right-side (knit) rows, even if your gauge specifies the increases to be worked on some wrong-side (purl) rows.

Work in stockinette and increase two stitches on every increase row (one at each side) until your total number of stitches equals the required number of stitches in the sleeve width. Stop increasing at this point. Continue to work in stockinette stitch until the sleeve measures required length. Bind off.

Machine knitting

Bottom edges of body and sleeves. Choose either a hemmed or ribbed bottom.

Hem—Bring forward the number of needles required. Start at the left edge and cast on the required number of stitches using a closed method. The yarn is now at the right. Thread the carriage. Set the stitch knob two sizes smaller than the size used to get the correct gauge. Work the inches of the hem. Set the stitch knob to the size used to get the correct gauge. Work the number of rows necessary for the desired hem length. Hang the bottom of the hem, stitch for stitch, onto the working needles.

Ribbing—Cast on the required number of stitches using a closed method. Set the stitch knob to two sizes smaller than that used to get the correct gauge. Work the required inches of ribbed band. Transfer the stitches from ribber to the main bed.

Body front and back. Set the stitch knob to the size used to get the correct gauge. Work the required number of rows to underarms. With the carriage at the right, bind off the appropriate number of underarm stitches at the left. Make one pass with the carriage. Bind off the appropriate number of underarm stitches at the right and make one pass with carriage. Work yoke for the required number of rows and bind off.

Sleeves. If using a hem, begin the increases on the row following hanging of the hem. If using a ribbed band, increase the stitch size and start the increases on the first row after the ribbed band is transferred to the main bed.

Increases—Place increases at least two stitches in from each edge as follows: Bring a new needle into working position on each edge; move the last two stitches of each edge over, leaving the third needle empty; on each side, bring up a stitch from the previous row, and hang it on the empty needle. Make one pass with the carriage. On each increase row you will have a total increase of two stitches.

Space your increase rows about one inch apart. (For example, If your gauge is 8 rows per inch, increase every 8th row.) Keep increasing until your total number of stitches equals the total required in the sleeve width. Stop increasing at that point and continue in stockinette stitch until the sleeve is the required length and bind off.

There are several ways to make the sleeve increases. Whichever method you choose, form the increases one or two stitches in from the edge stitch to keep the edges smooth and facilitate seam sewing.

Simple increase. The most common increase, at least among American knitters, is worked by knitting a stitch, retaining that stitch on the left needle, and then knitting into the back of the same stitch before slipping them both to the right needle. This results in a little horizontal bar on the face of the fabric.

Invisible increase. An easy, unobtrusive increase. Knit one stitch into the stitch of the last row, then knit the next stitch on the left needle.

Raised increase. Some designers designate this type of increase as "M 1". Using the left-hand needle, lift the horizontal thread between the two stitches that are on the two needles, and knit into it.

The Basic Sweater

■

Step Four: Finishing

Lightly steam, but do not iron, each piece, as you do not want the pieces to stretch. Machine-knitted pieces should be pulled into shape before steaming.

Lay the front and back pieces on a table, and sew front and back shoulders together. Unless you have added a little extra to the depth of the yoke for a shoulder seam allowance, use a joining technique that will allow the shoulders to butt-join, such as crocheting the edges together or using a lacing stitch. Leave a center opening large enough so the sweater will fit over the head—at least 10 inches wide for adults, 9 for children, and 8 for infants.

Sew the sleeves to the yoke. Sew bound-off underarm areas of the front and back to the sleeves. Fold sweater in half with right sides of front and back together. Sew arm and side seams. When sewing these seams, pass the needle from side to side catching the loops on the purl (wrong) side of the knitted fabric. This gives you a nice, flat seam with no bulky allowance. If you chose a hem finish, sew it in place.

Finish the neck with a single-stitch crochet or use a tapestry needle and work a buttonhole stitch around the neck edge.

That's all there is to making the Basic Sweater. In this version, it's a plain, one-color slipover with a straight boat neck. But think of all the easy ways to vary it; here are just a few:

—Choose a fancy yarn—tweedy, loopy, or fringed.

—Play color games: use a different color for the body, the yoke, the sleeves, the ribbings (see sweater on page 49). Or trade off two different colors of yarn for an all-over stripe (page 54).

—Use an all-over pattern stitch, such as seed stitch. Be sure to make your gauge samples in the pattern stitch instead of stockinette.

Butt-join with crochet

Lacing stitch

Catching loops on
purl side

There are several ways to sew seams. To avoid bulk, you can butt-join edges with crochet or attach two edges by passing a lacing stitch from side to side, catching the loops on the purl (wrong) side of the knitted fabric.

Simple Variations

The focus of this book is on understanding one basic, versatile sweater pattern, and then varying it to produce additional styles. Working with a basic pattern allows you to become familiar both with the procedure for making the sweater as well as how the completed sweater looks and fits.

This familiarity is helpful. How many times have you tried a new pattern only to wish, when it was finished, that you had done it a little differently? But, of course, there is no way to tell how a piece will actually look and fit until it is completed. Understanding the basic pattern thoroughly allows you to change it for future projects with minimum risk. It also allows you to repeat the parts that have proven successful while experimenting with others.

A simple V-neck

A very simple V-neck sweater that requires no picking up of stitches can be made by ribbing the entire yoke section. Construct the body front in the manner described in the basic pattern. Bind off the appropriate underarm stitches and divide the remaining yoke stitches into two equal groups. Work each side separately in a K1, P1 ribbing using the same size of needles or same stitch size used to get gauge. Work one side of the yoke for the combined length of both the front and back yokes. Then work the other side to match.

The neck looks best when both edges of the neck opening have the same stitch. If, for example, you ended with a purl at one side of the neck opening, then the other neck edge should start with a purl. It doesn't matter whether the neck edge stitch is a knit or purl. The point is that both edges look best when they are alike.

Once you have finished the two ribbed sections of the yoke, return to stockinette stitch, working all stitches as one row. Cast on the number of stitches needed for the underarms and work the body back down to the ribbed band. Change to smaller needles, or stitch size, and work ribbing (or hem). Bind off.

The sleeves are made the same as in the basic pattern. When the entire sweater is finished, sew a few inches of the center back yoke together by working back and forth and catching the knots at the edges of the rows.

A simple V-neck version of the Basic Sweater can be made by dividing the yoke in half and working each side separately in K1, P1 ribbing.

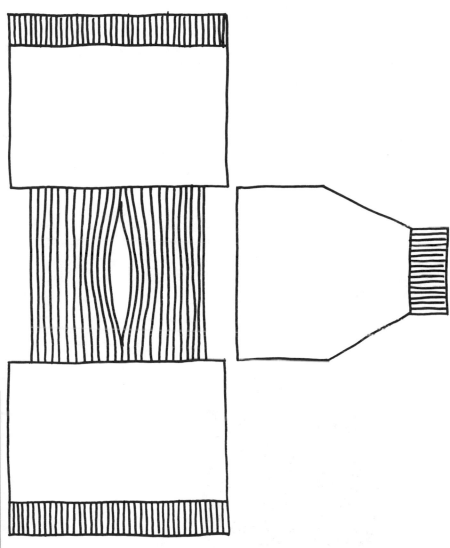

Simple Variations

■

▌ A simple saddle shoulder

This modification, which makes a nicely shaped neck opening that can be ribbed for a crew or turtle neckline, requires some reshaping of the yoke and sleeves. In this version, the yoke is made shorter and the center portion of each sleeve extends across the shoulders to the neckline.

As a rule of thumb, the width of the saddle is 4" for adults, 3" for children, and 2" for infants and toddlers. Thus, the yoke is knit three-fourths of its usual length (6 inches for an 8-inch yoke, 4½ inches for a 6-inch yoke, and 3 inches for a 4-inch yoke). The sleeves are worked as in the Basic Sweater to the required total length. Then an equal number of stitches on both edges are bound off, leaving a number of stitches equal to the width of the saddle. These saddle stitches are worked for about 5 inches in adult sizes, 3½ inches for children, and 2 inches for infants and toddlers.

For an 8-inch yoke sweater, for example, follow the basic pattern for the front and back to the point at which you have bound off the underarms and worked the yoke for a number of rows equal to 6 inches. (You should be within 2 inches of the top of the sweater.) Bind off an equal number of stitches on both outside edges, leaving 6 inches' worth of stitches in the center for the neck opening. Place these stitches on holders.

Knit the sleeves to the required total length. Bind off an equal number of stitches on both edges, leaving 4 inches' worth of stitches in the center. Work these center stitches for 5 inches. Place stitches on holders.

Sew all parts together as for the Basic Sweater. Remove holders from front, back, and sleeve stitches, and place these neck stitches onto double-pointed needles. Work K1, P1 ribbing by hand for the desired length.

A simple saddle shoulder version of the Basic Sweater can be made by shortening the yoke length and knitting extensions on the upper edges of the sleeves. This variation creates a square neck. Stitches left on the needles at the neck edges of the front, back, and sleeves can be worked in K1, P1 ribbing for a neckband. Note that the dimensions of the combined front and back yoke are unchanged (i.e., 16" by 16" on the 8-inch base pattern).)See also page 50.)

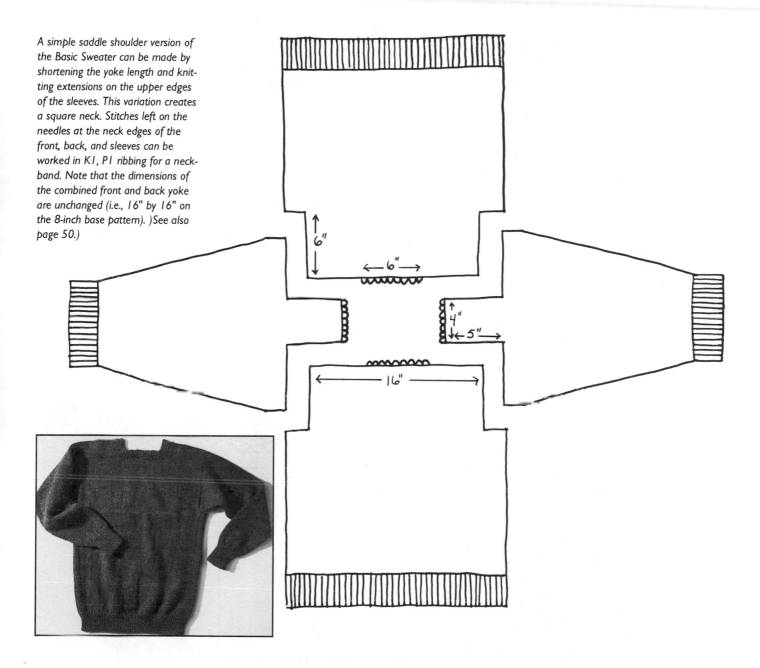

Simple Variations

■

Saddle shoulder with cables

This saddle shoulder version of the Basic Sweater has decorative cables running up each sleeve to the neckline. Use any cable you please, or try this simple 8-stitch one.

Place markers on each side of the center 8 stitches of each sleeve for the cables, and knit as follows: on right-side rows, P1, K6, P1. On wrong-side rows, K1, P6, K1. At the same time, on every eighth row (right side),

twist the cables as follows: P1, place next 3 stitches on cable needle and hold in front of work, K3, K3 stitches from cable needle, P1.

Because cables draw in more than plain stockinette stitch, it's important to make a generous sample first and adjust the number of stitches in the sleeve accordingly—adding about 2 stitches should compensate for the cable twist discussed here.

The saddle shoulder version can be modified with cables centered along each sleeve. Though cables have minimal effect on the number of rows per inch, they do cause the width to draw in more than in stockinette stitch. Therefore, if you plan to work a cable into your sleeve pattern, be sure to allow for this extra draw-in. Usually adding 2 to 4 stitches to the width will compensate, but work a generous sample to be sure.

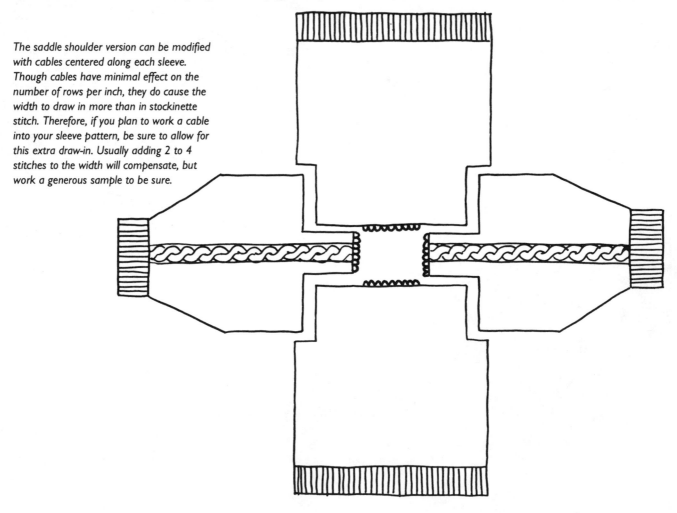

Expanding and contracting the yoke

The yoke can be expanded or contracted to produce interesting variations. This relatively simple modification is achieved by binding off fewer or more stitches at the underarms. However, there are a few considerations to keep in mind.

Binding off under the arms provides readily visible notches into which the sleeves are set. If the yoke is expanded to the full width of the sweater body (forming a dropped shoulder), this marking device no longer exists. So in this case, tie a strand of yarn at each point of the garment where the underarms would have been bound off so you can see just where to attach the sleeves.

The sleeve length depends in part on the width of the yoke. If you change the yoke width, be sure to note the new width on your Worksheet and calculate a new sleeve length accordingly.

Finally, if you are planning a pullover with a narrowed yoke, make sure you've allowed for a neck opening large enough to slip over the head.

expanded yoke

contracted yoke

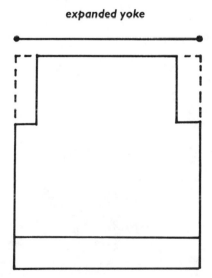
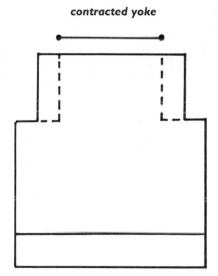

The yoke can be expanded or contracted by binding off fewer or more stitches at the underarm. If you choose to change the yoke width, be sure to adjust the sleeve length accordingly.

Simple Variations

■

Expanded Yoke

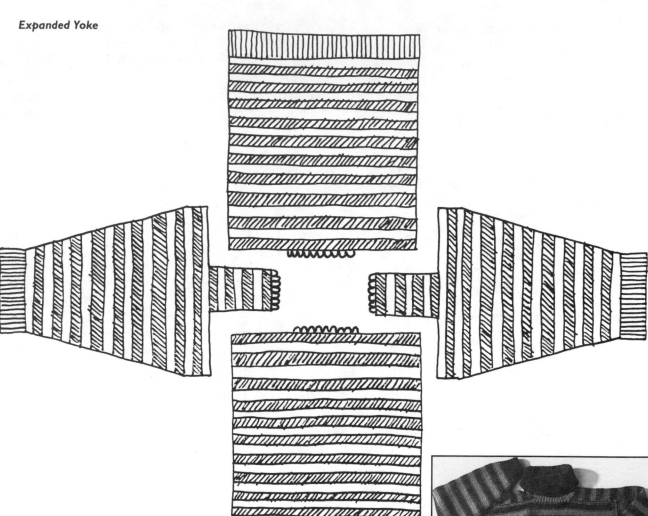

Contracted Yoke

Changing the yoke width can change the appearance of the Basic Sweater. Opposite: Expanded yoke on a saddle variation (see also page 51). This page: Contracted yoke on Basic Sweater (see also page 55). If you choose to contract the yoke, be sure the neck opening is wide enough to slip over the head.

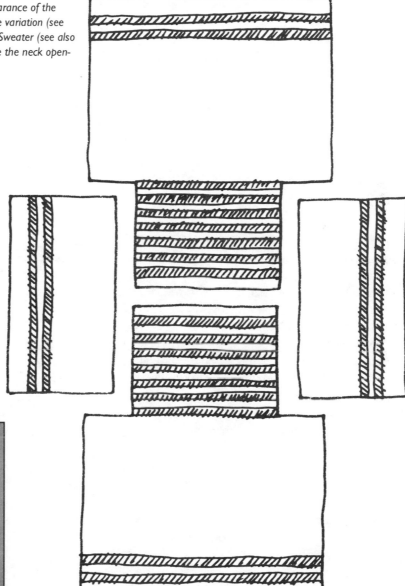

Having Fun with Gauged Graph Paper

Color motifs

The Basic Sweater is a perfect "blank canvas" for adding your own color designs; the rectangular yoke provides an unobstructed area in which to develop color motifs. Although shown in the working diagrams as a combination of squares, the yokes of the sweaters are knitted as continuous units. I've shown the yokes as squares to help you see how the large yoke area is composed of two or more smaller units. Color motifs, especially the ones based on repeat patterns, are much easier to design when they are broken down into such smaller units.

Just as these yokes can be broken down into two or four parts, they can also be broken down into even smaller units. The 6-inch base yoke can be broken down into horizontal bands, 3-inch squares, and 2-inch squares, to name a few. Similar configurations can be made for all other yoke sizes.

To design a patterned yoke for any size of the Basic Sweater, start by making several photocopies of the Planning Guide provided at the back of this book. Think of the Planning Guide as your doodling paper. Take a pencil and fill in some of the squares with repeat patterns. Even if you think you're not artistic, you can come up with an amazing number of interesting designs, just a few of which are shown on pages 42 and 43.

Use colored pencils to get an idea of how the motif will look in color. By using colors that approximate those of the yarns you plant to use in a proposed project, you can get a fairly good idea of how the motif will look when it is knitted.

To knit one of these simple diagonal motifs, or any other design you come up with, you can use photocopies of the Gauged Graph Papers in the back of this book to make a stitch-by-stitch knitting pattern. Why Gauged Graph Paper, with its oblong divisions, instead of the usual even-squared graph paper? On the Gauged Graph Papers, one square equals one stitch. If you look at your knitted fabric closely, you'll see that each stitch is just a little wider than it is tall. In some pattern stitches, this difference is extreme. Thus, a design graphed on regular square graph paper will look flattened when knitted up, as in the circle motif on page 45.

To eliminate this distortion, I've devised the 20

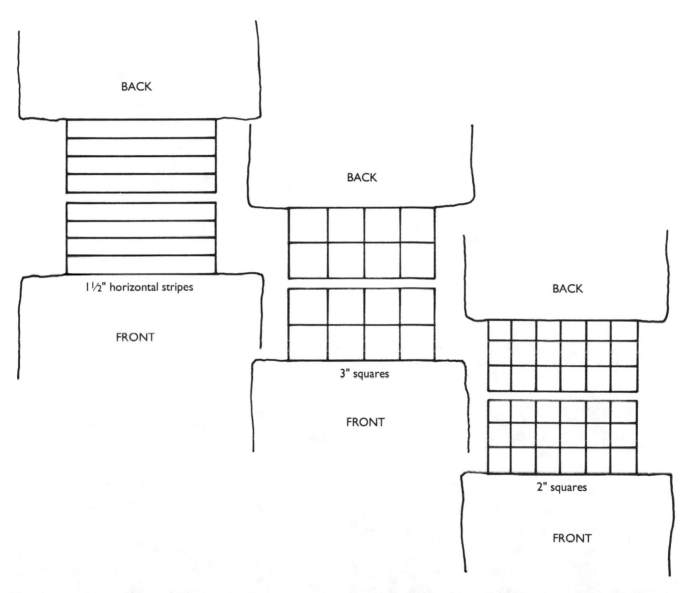

BACK

1½" horizontal stripes

FRONT

BACK

3" squares

FRONT

BACK

2" squares

FRONT

The yoke area of the sweater can be broken down into smaller parts. Here the 6-inch base yoke is shown broken into three configurations. You can plan motifs to fit in these smaller units.

Gauged Graph Paper

■

diagonal key

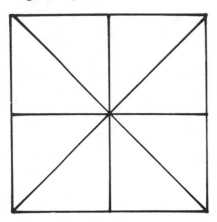

Make a diagonal key by ruling vertical, horizontal, and diagonal lines on a 2-inch square. On the appropriate Graph Paper, pick and choose the squares that best represent the diagonal lines. Once you've plotted the diagonals, you can build upon this 2-inch square to make larger motifs.

4 x 5 key

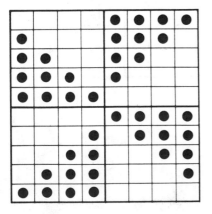

5 x 7 key

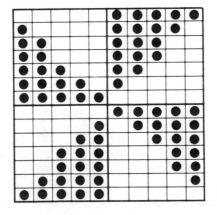

6 x 8 key

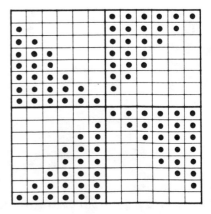

Gauged Graph Papers here to represent the most common combinations of stitches per inch and rows per inch. If you choose the Gauged Graph Paper that corresponds to your gauge to chart your motif, you will be able to see exactly how it will look knitted up.

The simplest motifs to design are those based on intersecting vertical and horizontal lines. To incorporate diagonal lines, you'll need to devise a diagonal key. To do so, mark off a 2-inch by 2-inch area on the appropriate Gauged Graph Paper. Using a straight edge, rule in diagonals from corner to corner. Now pick and choose the squares of the graph paper that best represent your diagonal lines. Once you've found the squares that best fit the diagonal, you can build upon this 2-inch square to make larger motifs (see pages 46 and 47).

Adding a third color might complicate the knitting process (see intarsia knitting on page 75), but it can add a fascinating dimensional look to simple geometric motifs. (In order to maintain your gauge, it's important that all of the colors of yarn be of the same yarn type. Mixing different yarns may result in gauge distortions and differential shrinkage.)

Gauged Graph Paper is also an excellent aid in charting patterns for motifs based on curved lines. Even if the Graph Paper doesn't match your gauge exactly, it's much more in proportion than the same motif graphed on ordinary squared graph paper.

To graph a free-form motif, draw around the number of inches that you wish to devote to the motif on a copy of the appropriate Gauged Graph Paper. Using plain paper, sketch the desired shape until you get it just right. Tape the free-form drawing to a window, tape the Graph Paper over it, and transfer the shape to the Graph Paper. (Or use a light table if you have one.) Shade in the area that best represents your design. It may take you several attempts to achieve just the right shape. Once you have a shape you like, take a fresh photocopy of Graph Paper and carefully designate each stitch in your design with dots or other symbols. This then becomes your working pattern.

When you've come up with a motif that you like, tape several copies of the Gauged Graph Paper together and outline the appropriate number of stitches and rows in your yoke area (see your Worksheet). You can now chart motifs directly on the paper and see exactly how they will work up in the sweater.

There's no end to the possible sources for motif ideas. Transfer a child's drawing to your Graph Paper, or a name or favorite motto, or a simple landscape. Mine the many wonderful books of charted patterns for cross-stitchers and needlepointers, not to mention knitters. Of course, you may have to adjust these motifs to allow for the flattened effect of knit stitches, and you'll also have to consider how many colors you want to carry in each row, or how many bobbins you want to work with to accommodate frequent color changes. But with plenty of copies of your Planning Guide and Graph Paper at hand, you can adjust and play with your design until it's perfect.

Working out charted motifs is not always easy. Sometimes it takes several tries to develop a pleasing shape. This is particularly true of designs composed of curved lines. Once completed, a graphed shape looks easy, but that is because you are looking only at the finished product. For each successful motif that you create, there are usually many that did not look quite right and were discarded. So, once you've developed a motif that you're pleased with, don't hesitate to use it again and again.

Reusing motifs and basic patterns does not mean, however, that you are simply making a lot of items that look alike. Once you are familiar with a basic pattern, you can then go on to experiment within the familiar and define shapes to produce a multitude of variations—

Gauged Graph Paper

■

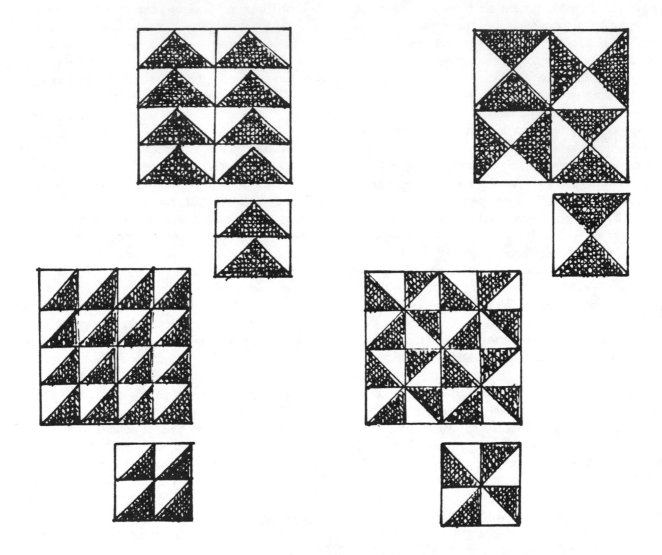

Use the Planning Guide to sketch repeat patterns to knit into your sweater. The pattern possibilities are limitless—just a few are shown here. A master copy of the Planning Guide is included at the back of this book. Make photocopies of the master for your sketches.

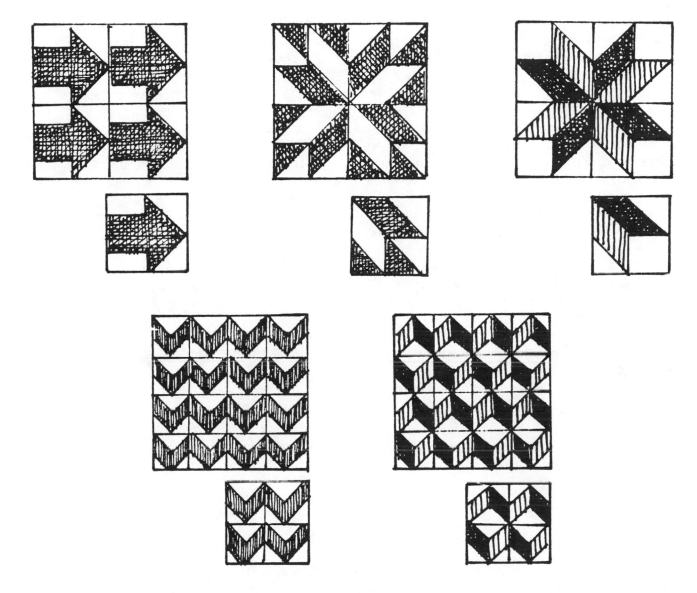

Gauged Graph Paper

■

none of which need to look alike.

Having a few good basic patterns also allows you to use ideas from the many needlework books that contain a great deal of technique information, but no patterns. Using the Basic Sweater Pattern, you can transform the technical material supplied in these other books into finished pieces of your own design.

While the yoke area is an obvious location for color motifs, you can use your Gauged Graph Paper to make designs for other parts of the sweater, too. Try some of these motifs on the sleeves, or arrange them over the entire sweater. Once you have mastered the technique, it's easy. Just be sure to pay attention to how the design looks when all the pieces are put together—you'll know for sure if you've charted out the entire sweater on Gauged Graph Paper.

In the event that none of the accompanying Gauged Graph Papers matches your gauge exactly, you have some options:

1. If it is a matter of a slight difference, knit a new swatch, making it either tighter or looser, until it corresponds to one of the provided Graph Papers. You will need to go back and recalculate the number of stitches and rows on your Worksheet before you begin to knit your sweater.

2. Pick the paper that most closely approximates your gauge. Disregard the inch markings, and simply designate the required number of stitches and rows represented by your gauge.

For example, imagine that your gauge is six stitches per inch and nine rows per inch and you want to diagram a 4-inch-square area. Though there is no 6 × 9 gauged paper, you can modify the 6 × 8 paper. The six stitch divisions per inch would remain the same, but there would be 36, and not 32, rows in 4 inches. You can simply draw a line at the 36-row mark and adjust your motif to fit in this area. While the resulting diagram is slightly distorted, it is much more in proportion than if you had used squared (such as 8 × 8) paper.

3. It is also possible to modify the papers. For instance, if the gauged paper has one-half the stitches and rows per inch as your gauge, you can simply use a ruler and divide each square in half both vertically and horizontally.

Circle motif plotted on square graph paper

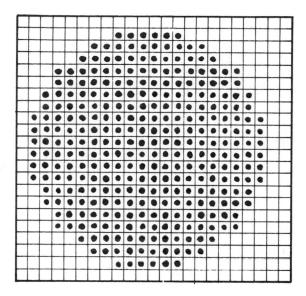

Motif knitted at a gauge of 5 stitches and 7 rows per inch

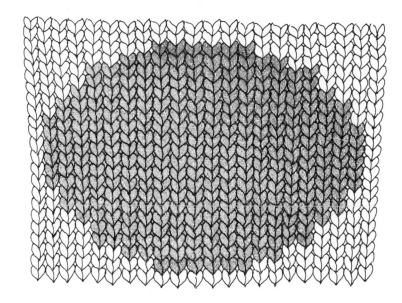

Because knit stitches are slightly wider than they are long, a motif drawn on square graph paper will appear squashed when knitted up. If the same motif is drawn on the appropriate Gauged Graph Paper, it will knit up exactly as drawn.

Gauged Graph Paper

■

6 x 8

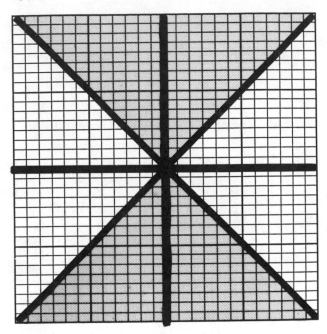

Use the diagonal key to determine the squares (stitches) that best fit diagonal lines on the appropriate Graph Paper. You can make a number of distinctly different motifs by simply changing the orientation of the shaded areas.

6 x 8

4 x 5

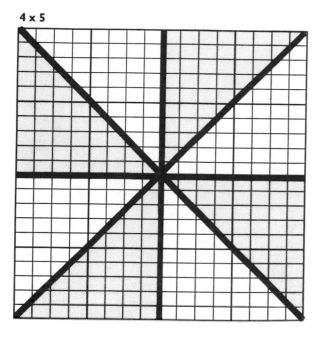

4 x 5

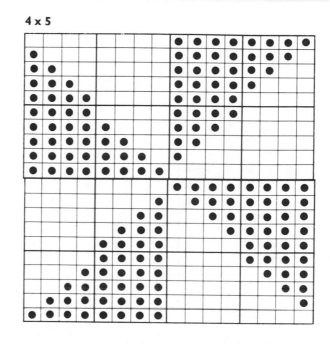

5 x 7

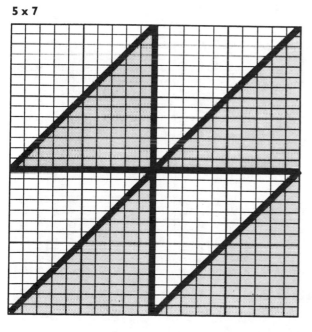

5 x 7

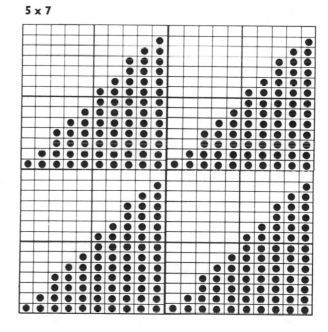

Gauged Graph Paper

■

4 x 5

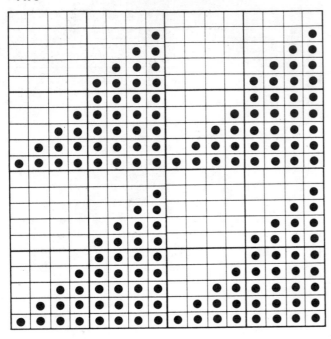

Your gauge will determine which squares best represent a diagonal line. A motif worked out for one gauge must be slightly modified to work for another, as shown in these examples.

5 x 7

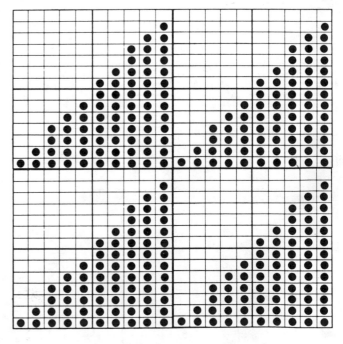

A simple variation on the Basic Sweater—knit
the body, yoke, sleeves, and ribbings in contrasting colors. Or for a dressier look, try shades of
white in contrasting textures—silky, nubby, and
fuzzy.

Bold geometric motifs are easy to plot
on Gauged Graph Paper and knit into
the Basic Sweater.

The Basic Sweater can be modified with saddle shoulders, automatically creating a crew-neck shape.

*Bold stripes accentuate the saddle shoulder
shaping of this version of the Basic Sweater.
The turtle neck is simply a crew-neck ribbing
that didn't quit.*

The Basic Sweater yoke is a perfect "blank canvas" for knitting in graphed motifs.

The Planning Guide and Gauged Graph Paper make geometric motifs a breeze. In this version of the Basic Sweater, stripes on the body and sleeves pick up the colors of the yoke design.

53

A double-breasted cardigan in seed stitch. The ribbed yoke contracts for built-in shaping.

The Basic Sweater goes to great lengths. Picoted hems add design interest to the body and sleeve edges.

The Basic Sweater in fine pastel stripes teams up for a "layered look".

A crew-neck cardigan variation of the Basic Sweater has extra-long sleeve ribbing and oversize buttons.

Parade

"School Bus Sweater", a V-neck cardigan variation of the Basic Sweater, was adapted from original wall art (see page 56).

Reverse stockinette stitch and heart-shaped buttons give this V-neck cardigan a perky look.

Add a simple straight skirt with picoted hem to match a short-sleeved version of the Basic Sweater for a hand- or machine-knitted ensemble.

A hood and logo give a crew-neck version of the Basic Sweater a collegiate look.

You can tape together enough pieces of Gauged Graph Paper to draw a whole sweater—neck shaping, charted motifs, and all.

The "School Bus Sweater" was adapted from a work entitled "Here Comes the School Bus". The motifs were easy to convert into a knitting pattern using Gauged Graph Paper. Duplicate stitch, buttons, and embroidery provide the smaller details.

4 x 5

5 x 7

Your gauge will determine which squares best represent a diagonal line. A motif worked out for one gauge must be slightly modified to work for another, as shown in these examples.

Gauged Graph Paper

■

4 x 5

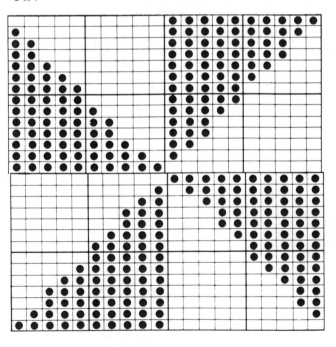

5 x 7

4 x 5

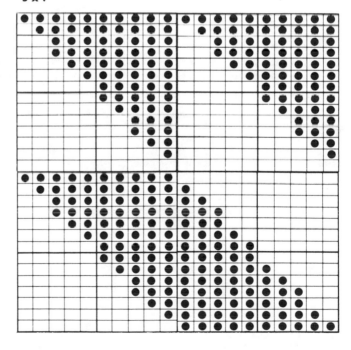

All of these motifs are based on the same diagonal line. Rotating the motif in space gives a number of different designs.

5 x 7

Gauged Graph Paper

■

4 x 5

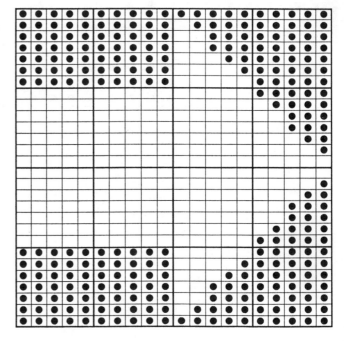

Combine horizontal, vertical, and diagonal lines to make arrow motifs.

5 x 7

Adding a third color might complicate the knitting process, but can add dimension to a motif.

Gauged Graph Paper

■

While the Gauged Graph Paper is ideal for working out diagonal and free-form motifs, don't forget that simple horizontal stripes can add interest too. You can make your sweater design look much more complicated by adding stripes to the sleeves and body in the same colors as used in the yoke motif. Use the appropriate Gauged Graph Paper to plan stripe placement if you want the stripes on the sleeves to fall in a continuous line with the stripes on the body front and back.

The pinwheel motif on this sweater (see also page 53) was worked out using vertical, horizontal, and diagonal lines on 4.5 x 6 Graph Paper for a 10-inch base yoke. Colorful stripes were added just below the armhole of the body and sleeves.

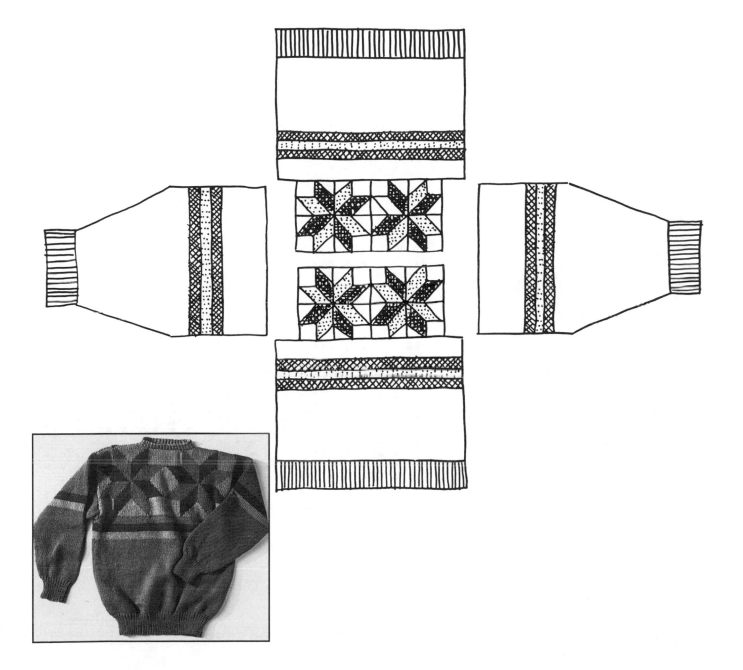

Gauged Graph Paper

6 x 8

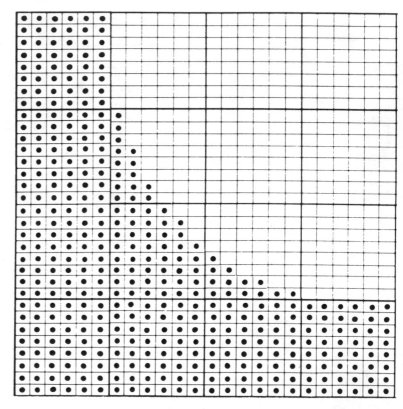

Curved or free-form motifs can also be plotted on Gauged Graph Paper. As with motifs composed of diagonal lines, the squares that best represent a curved form depend on your gauge.

5 x 7

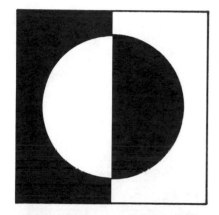

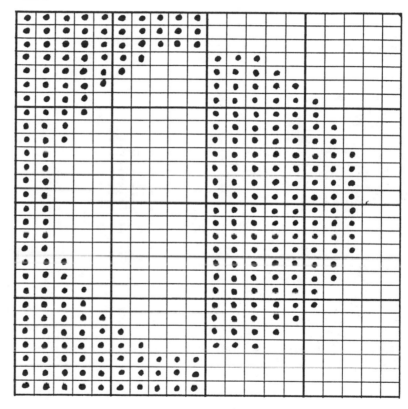

Gauged Graph Paper

■

5 x 7

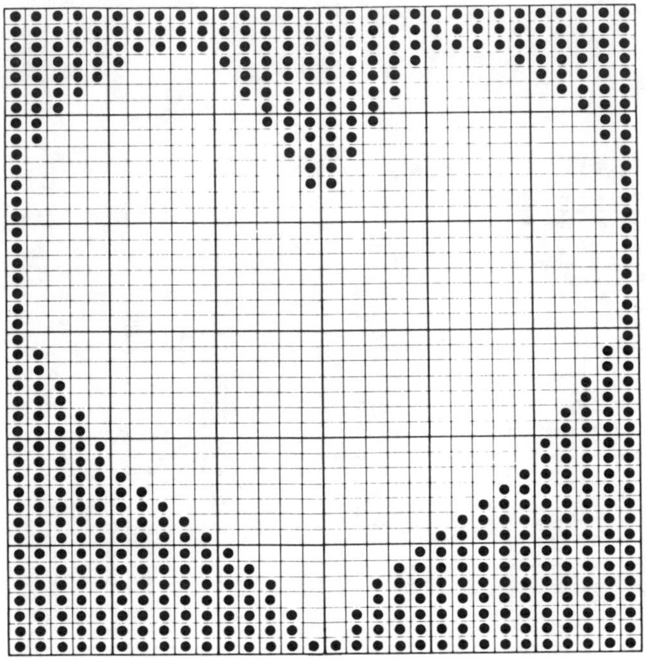

Hearts take a little more planning.

6 x 8

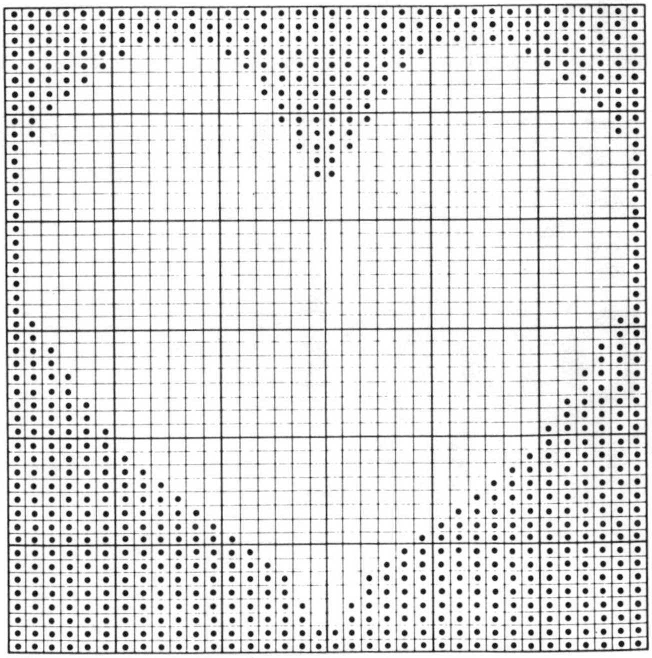

5 x 7

6 x 8

You can alter the appearance of a motif by reversing the placement of dark and light colors.

Gauged Graph Paper

■

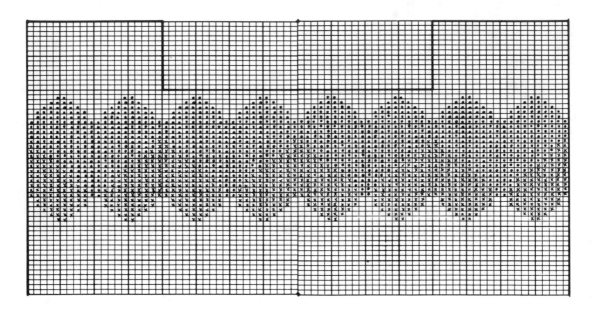

To see exactly how motifs will work up in a sweater, tape together enough copies of the appropriate Graph Paper to accommodate the entire yoke area and plot your motif. You can use colored pencils to approximate the colors of yarn you plan to use. The yoke on the simple saddle shoulder version of the Basic Sweater pictured opposite was worked in four separate squares which were later sewn together. A version that was knitted in one piece is shown on page 52.

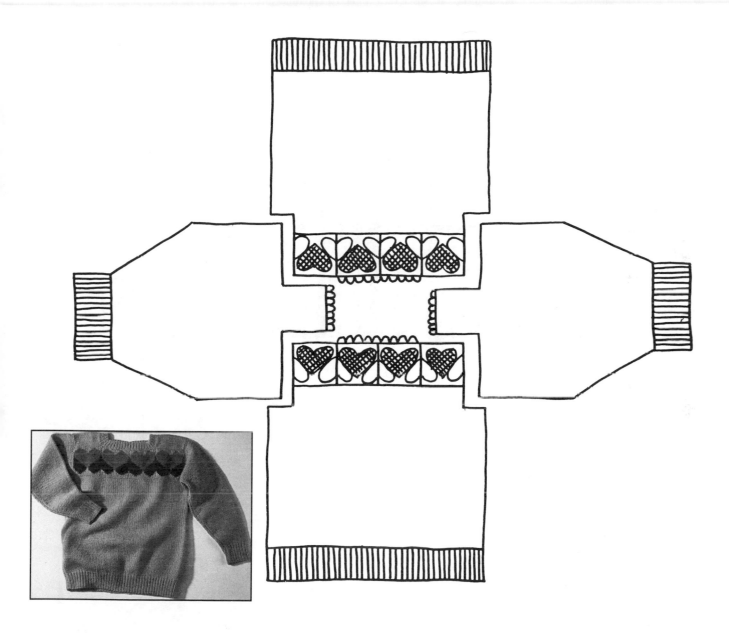

Gauged Graph Paper

■

There's no end to the possible motifs that can be worked into your sweater. Plot a drawing, a name or motto, or a simple landscape on the appropriate Graph Paper and then transfer it to your sweater as you knit.

4.5 x 6

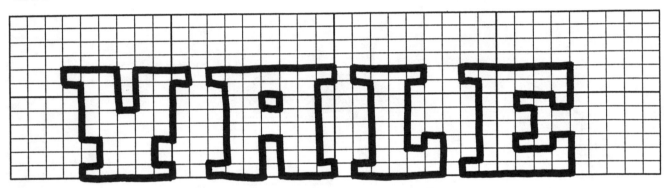

4.5 x 6

5 x 7

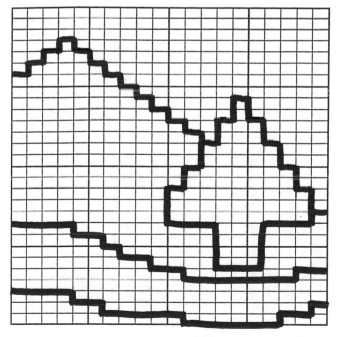

Gauged Graph Paper

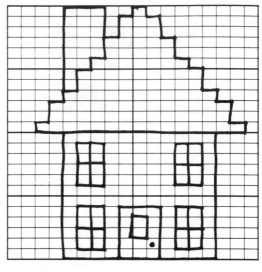

4.5 x 6

4.5 x 6

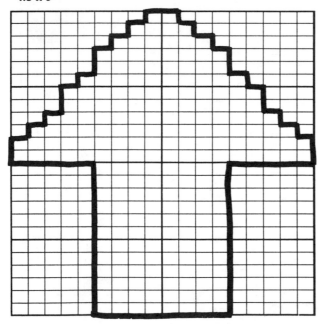

4.5 x 6

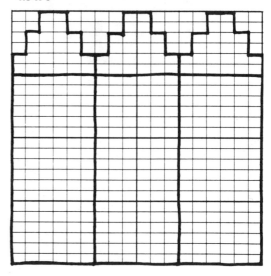

A basic motif can be modified to produce similar but different shapes. Here, an arrow motif is adapted to form house and crayon shapes.

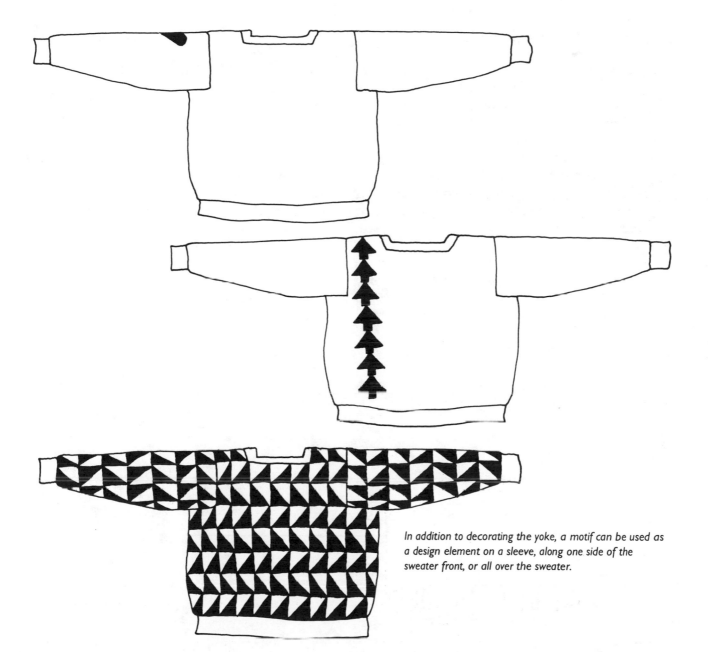

In addition to decorating the yoke, a motif can be used as a design element on a sleeve, along one side of the sweater front, or all over the sweater.

Gauged Graph Paper
■

Incorporating stitch patterns

Decorative or textural stitches can be incorporated into the Basic Sweater just as easily as color motifs can. The first step is to knit a sample swatch using the yarn and stitch pattern that you plan to use for your sweater. Carefully measure the new swatch to determine the number of stitches and rows per inch of knitted fabric. You'll find that the gauge for different stitches can vary widely from that of stockinette knitted with the same yarn and needles. Use your gauge information, along with your measurements and the Worksheet, to calculate your working pattern.

Working out stitch patterns can become as involved as devising color motifs. A pattern stitch, such as the seed stitch, poses few difficulties; however, intricate stitch designs such as all-over cables can be problemat-

ical. Not only do these stitches change your gauge significantly, they also are based on a specific number of stitches per repeat which must be taken into account when you determine the number of stitches to use for the body width.

If you choose to use a pattern stitch in hand knitting, make a sample swatch much larger than usual—perhaps 10 inches square. You can simplify matters by confining the patterned portion of the body front and back to an area that is about the same width as the yoke. This facilitates the transition from the body to the yoke, and leaves a narrow strip down each lower body edge that is worked in stockinette stitch. These unpatterned areas along each edge of the sweater help to resolve differences between the number of stitches required in a design repeat and the number of inches in the width of your garment.

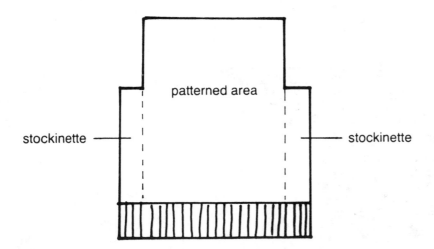

stockinette — patterned area — stockinette

If you choose to use a stitch design that is composed of multiple stitches, confine the design to an area that is roughly equivalent to the yoke width. Use stockinette stitch on the edges to help resolve differences between the number of stitches required in a pattern repeat and the number of inches needed in the width of your garment.

Knitting from your graphed designs

In hand knitting, color patterns are created using either color stranding (also called Fair Isle), or intarsia (also called argyle) techniques.

Color stranding is the best technique for knitting designs that require a lot of frequent color changes. To do color stranding, carry two (or more) strands of yarn in contrasting colors along as you knit or purl instead of the usual single strand. Use one or the other of the yarns to make each stitch, according to what your chart or pattern indicates, carrying the unused yarn in back of your work.

If a color must be carried for a long distance, say for five or more stitches, stop and twist the two yarns together every few stitches to prevent long, loose floats on the back. Some effective techniques for making color stranding quick and efficient are detailed in Jacqueline Fee's *Sweater Workshop* (Interweave Press, 1983), and many other basic knitting books.

Intarsia knitting is most appropriate for the bold, blocky patterns used in most of the sweaters in this book. It's how argyle socks, with their large, solid diamonds of color, have been traditionally knitted.

To do intarsia, make a small mini-skein of yarn for each different color area in your pattern. As you work across each row, change yarns wherever your Graph Paper chart indicates, leaving the unused yarns hanging down in back of your work, ready to be picked up on the next row. As you change colors, twist the new yarn *under and around* the old one to prevent holes in your work. Barbara Abbey's *Complete Book of Knitting* (Viking Press, 1974) describes this technique in detail.

How you execute color patterns by machine depends entirely upon the kind of knitting machine that you own. Some machines have pattern card devices. Executing one of these graphed designs on such a machine requires making a new pattern card. Some knitting machines produce intarsia patterns by having the yarn laid across the needles by hand and/or by using an intarsia yarn feeder.

Before beginning to knit projects using more than one color, refer to your machine manual or hand knitting reference book for specific directions on how to knit intarsia patterns. Then practice, practice, practice the technique described until you have mastered the basic procedures.

Using the Gauged Graph Paper for Advanced Shape Modifications

The Gauged Graph Paper is useful for more than working out color patterns. It's also the best tool you have for working out neck shapes and cardigan openings. There are many ways to restyle the parts of the Basic Sweater to create garments that look completely different. Many ideas can be gleaned from looking at commercial garments as well as hand- and machine-made sweaters in needlework books and magazines.

Shaped necks

Square necks, round necks, and V-necks of varying widths and depths can all be charted on the appropriate Gauged Graph Paper. First figure how wide and long the neck opening is to be. As a rule of thumb, I use 6 inches in width for adults, 5 inches for children, and 4 inches for infants and toddlers. The depth of the neck back and front can vary depending on the look you want, or the shape of the wearer. I often bind off the neck back at the same time as the shoulders. If you want more shaping in the back, allow 1–2 inches for adults, ¾–1½ inches for children, and ½–1 inch for toddlers.

The depth of the neck front depends on the overall shape you choose. You can relate the depth of a front neck opening to the yoke size of the particular sweater. For example, I often start V-neck shaping on the same row on which the underarms are bound off. If, however, you want the depth of the finished V-neck to correspond to the underarm area, then begin the V-neck shaping an inch below the underarm bind-off row. When ribbing is added, the finished opening will then be as deep as the underarm.

Crew neck. For the front of a crew or round neck, I often use necks that are 2–4 inches deep for adults, 1½–3 inches deep for children, and 1–2 inches deep for infants and toddlers. Keep in mind that these are only approximations. The most important thing to remember is that these types of necks must be large enough to slip over the head. You should determine this on an individual project basis.

When you've determined the width and length of your neck opening, sketch it lightly on the appropriate Gauged Graph Paper (tape together enough photocop-

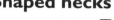
6 x 8

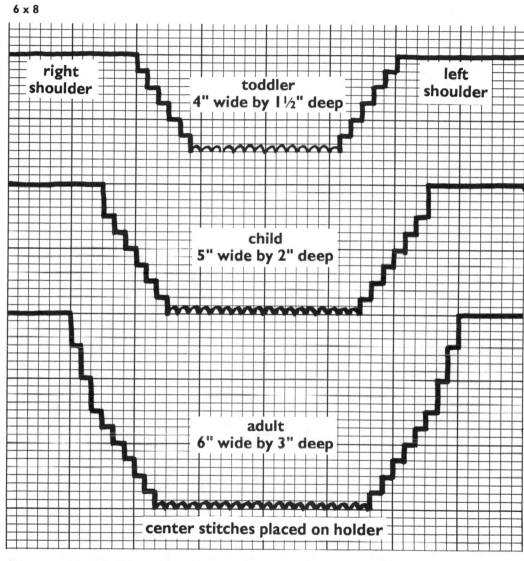

Rounded or crew front neck shapings plotted on 6 x 8 Graph Paper for adult, child, and toddler sweaters. Suggested neck openings that are to be finished with ribbing are: 6 inches wide by 2–4 inches deep for adults; 5 inches wide by 1½–3 inches deep for children; 4 inches wide by 1–2 inches deep for infants and toddlers. Just one possible configuration for each size is shown here—use the appropriate Gauged Graph Paper to work out other shapes.

Advanced Shape Modifications

■

6 x 8

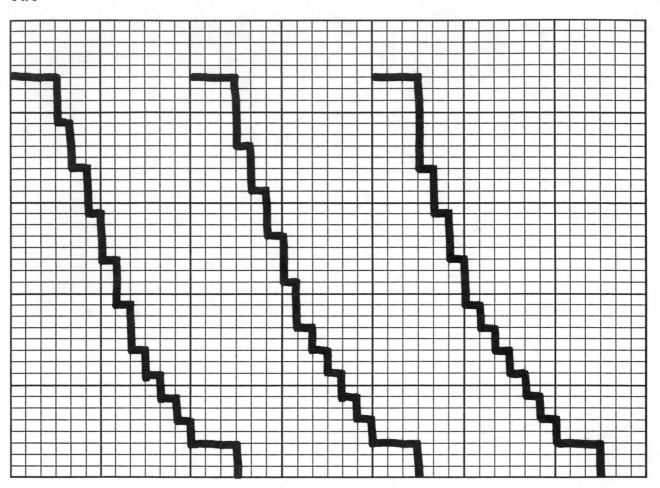

There are several ways to achieve a rounded neck shape. Here are three ways to decrease 12 stitches in 32 rows.

This crew-neck version of the Basic Sweater has extra long sleeve ribbing. The same shaping was used for both the front and back neck and the neck stitches were worked into a hood (see page 85). The letters on the yoke were worked out on Graph Paper. See also page 55.

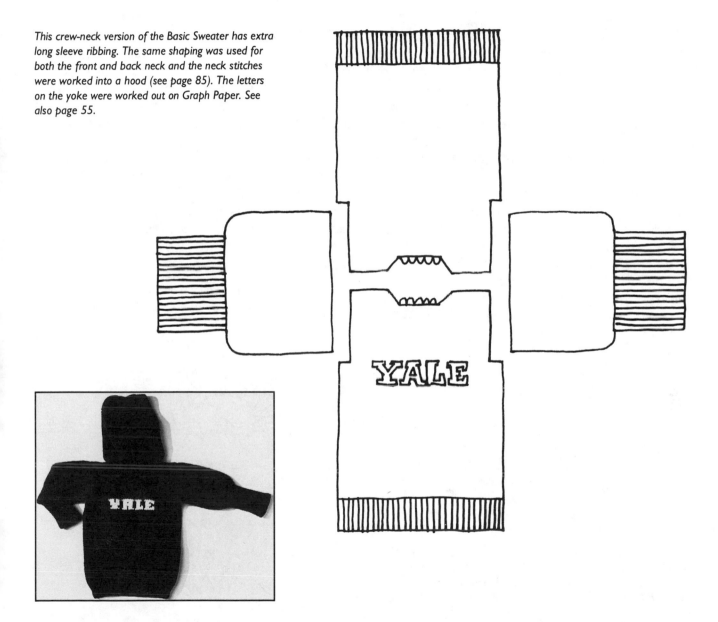

Advanced Shape Modifications

■

ies of Graph Paper to equal the size of the yoke area) and then try various sequences of decreases to see which works best. There are always several ways to accomplish the required number of decreases, each resulting in a slightly different shape. Once you've drawn a shape onto the Gauged Graph Paper and devised several possible ways to achieve it, it is you, the designer, who must make the final decision. Whatever you decide to do will be the correct answer.

Charted instructions indicate the row on which an increase or decrease will occur; however, the chart does not tell you where to place the increase or decrease. The decrease can be placed on the edge stitch, or it may be appropriate to place it one or two stitches in from the edge. When a particular notation reads, "Decrease 1 stitch at the neck edge every other row," it simply indicates that the decrease should be made somewhere within the 3 or 4 edge stitches.

V-neck. For a shaped V-neck in an adult garment using the 8-inch yoke, I often plan an opening in the center front that is 6 inches wide (at the top) and 9 inches long. For a child's garment, using the 6-inch yoke, the V-shaped opening might be 5 inches wide (at the top) and 7½ inches long. For a toddler, dimensions might be 4 inches wide by 6 inches long.

Keep in mind that the neck shape you've charted is usually not complete in itself. Shaped necks are typically finished with a ribbed band or some other trim, so you need to allow for its addition as you plan. To obtain a ribbing that lies flat on a V-neck shaping, refer to one of the general knitting books listed in the bibliography on page 102.

Sl 1, k 1, psso

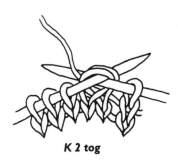

K 2 tog

ssk

*The simplest decrease is **K 2 tog**, or knit two stitches together. This creates a decrease which slants to the right. To match it with a left-slanting decrease, slip one knitwise, knit one, and pass the slipped stitch over the knit stitch (**psso**). Another way to make a left-leaning decrease is to slip-slip-knit (**ssk**), for which you slip a stitch knitwise, slip a second stitch knitwise, and then insert the left needle into those two stitches and knit them off as one. This is close to being a mirror image of K 2 tog.*

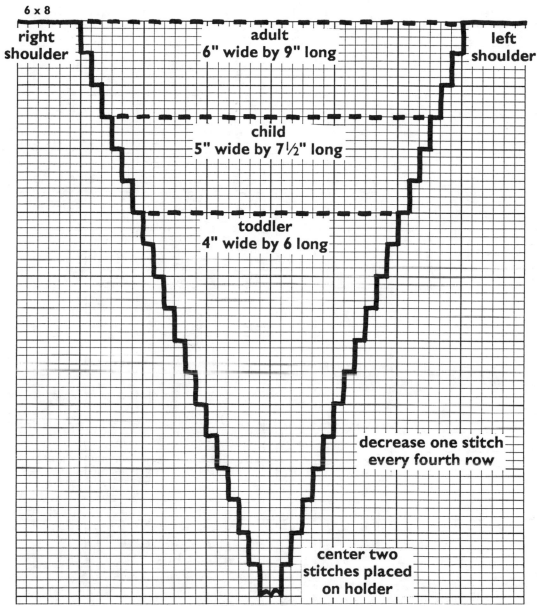

6 x 8

right shoulder

adult 6" wide by 9" long

left shoulder

child 5" wide by 7½" long

toddler 4" wide by 6 long

decrease one stitch every fourth row

center two stitches placed on holder

V-neck front and back neck shapings for adult, child, and toddler sweaters. A standard V-neck for adults is 6 inches wide by 9 inches long; for children, 5 inches wide by 7½ inches long; for toddlers, 4 inches wide by 6 inches long. The rate of decrease will depend on your gauge—plot it out on the appropriate Gauged Graph Paper. For a 6 x 8 gauge, you could decrease one stitch every fourth row.

Advanced Shape Modifications

■

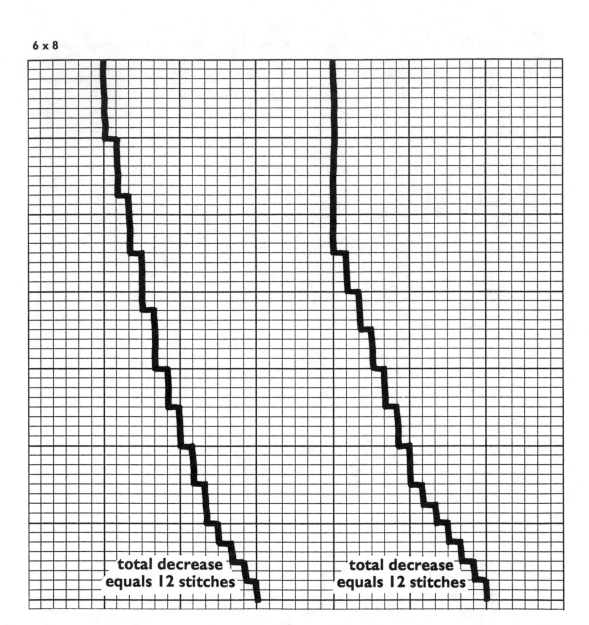

6 x 8

total decrease
equals 12 stitches

total decrease
equals 12 stitches

Here are two possible ways to decrease 12 stitches over a 7-inch length on 6 x 8 Graph Paper. Though the number of decreases is the same, the resulting shapes are quite different. The shapes would be different still if the same decreases were worked out on Graph Paper keyed to a different gauge. It's up to you, the designer, to decide the shape that's best for your garment.

Cardigans

To make a cardigan, you must knit two front mirror-image sections, each half as wide as the front of the Basic Sweater. The simplest cardigan is the saddle shoulder version, for it requires no neck shaping and no picking up of stitches. A separating zipper can be used as a front closure so that overlapping bands are also avoided.

Once the parts are knitted and sewed together, the neck stitches (which have been placed on holders) can be knitted up to form a crew neck, a collar, or a hood. A crew neck is knitted in ribbing for about 1 inch. Lengthening the ribbing creates a collar. And lengthening the collar and seaming it at the top makes a hood.

If you want a sweater that buttons, you'll need to calculate the dimensions of the button and buttonhole bands. First decide how wide the bands should be. The obvious starting point is to choose your buttons. The oversized buttons on the sweaters on pages 54 and 55 are major design elements, and required more than an average width (i.e., 1-inch-wide) button band. If you wait until the knitting is completed and then go to the fabric shop to buy buttons, you may find that the buttons you like don't work within the dimensions of your sweater.

Measure the diameter of your buttons and plan bands just a little bit wider. The bands overlap along the center line, so plan to make each band extend past the center line of each sweater front by half of its width.

Button and buttonhole bands can either be knitted simultaneously with each section of the garment front, or stitches can be picked up along the center front of each piece and the bands worked during the finishing phase. In our culture, buttons and buttonholes have gender associations. That is to say, for women buttons are placed on the left front of a garment and the buttonholes are located on the right front. For men, the positions are reversed. I have always thought this a curious differentiation; however, it may serve as an aid for those who have difficulty distinguishing men from women. Whatever the case, this means that for a proper sweater you must decide for whom the garment is intended and designate the button and buttonhole sides accordingly.

The actual placement of buttons and buttonholes occurs during the knitting process. First knit the button side (or button band) of the garment, then lay the buttons out on the finished piece as you want them to be spaced. Measure the spacings to determine which rows should have buttonholes. Then knit the other side (or band), making buttonholes in the correct locations as you go.

Advanced Shape Modifications

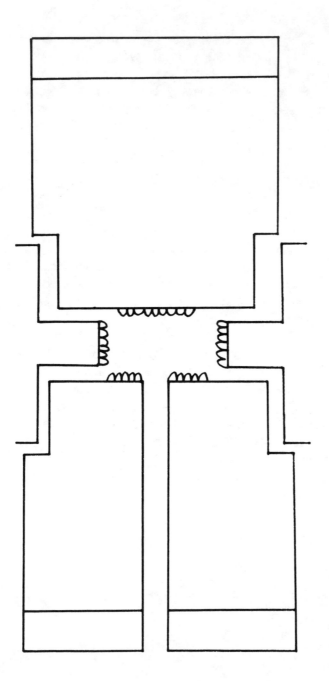

The saddle shoulder version of the Basic Sweater can be made into a cardigan by working the front in two sections. If a separating zipper is used for the front closure, no overlapping bands need to be added. Be sure to knit the two front sections as mirror images of each other.

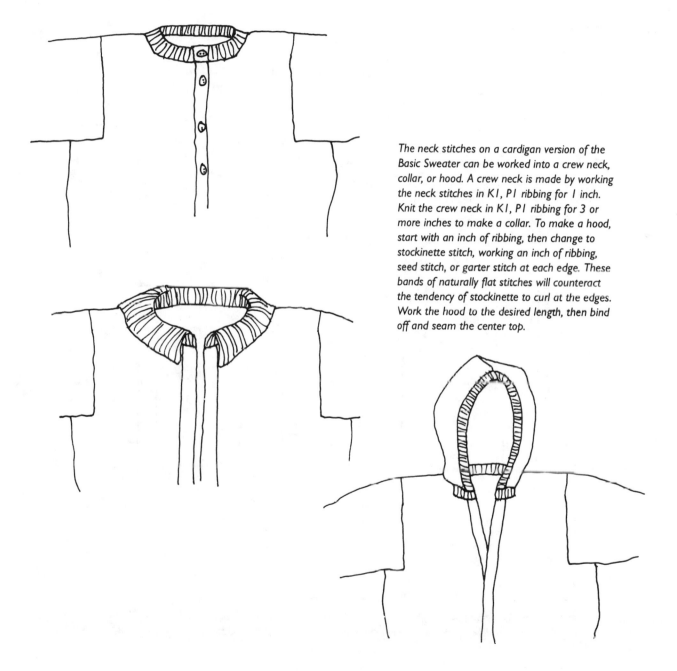

The neck stitches on a cardigan version of the Basic Sweater can be worked into a crew neck, collar, or hood. A crew neck is made by working the neck stitches in K1, P1 ribbing for 1 inch. Knit the crew neck in K1, P1 ribbing for 3 or more inches to make a collar. To make a hood, start with an inch of ribbing, then change to stockinette stitch, working an inch of ribbing, seed stitch, or garter stitch at each edge. These bands of naturally flat stitches will counteract the tendency of stockinette to curl at the edges. Work the hood to the desired length, then bind off and seam the center top.

Advanced Shape Modifications
■

A crew-neck cardigan

Suppose you want to knit a 40-inch-circumference crew-neck cardigan with a 3-inch band of ribbing at the waist and 2-inch-wide ribbed button and buttonhole bands that are picked up during the finishing phase. If the total circumference of the sweater is 40 inches, the original front width is 20 inches. For a cardigan, this width is divided into two fronts, each 10 inches wide. To calculate the stockinette part of the body fronts, subtract the overlapping part of the band (1 inch) from the original body width (10 inches):

10 inches − 1 inch = 9 inches

Each front section, then, consists of 9 inches of stockinette. The bottom 3 inches of the waist is knitted in ribbing, then the rest of the body in stockinette. The neck decreases are plotted on graph paper, and that becomes the knitting pattern. Once they have been knitted, the front and back sections are joined at the shoulders and the crew-neck ribbing is knitted. Finally, stitches for the button and buttonhole bands are picked up along the entire front sections from neck to waist and knitted in K1, P1 ribbing for 2 inches.

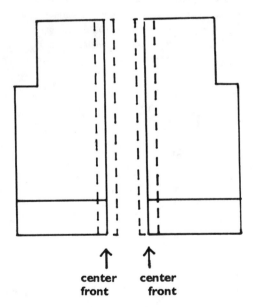

center
front

center
front

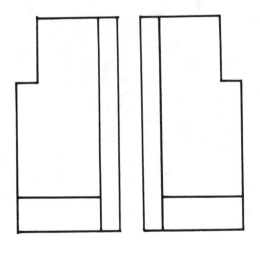

Add overlapping bands for a cardigan that buttons. The width of the bands depends on the size buttons you choose. The bands should be centered about the center line of each front and one-half of the band width subtracted from the width of the body. The bands overlap a distance equal to one-half of their width.

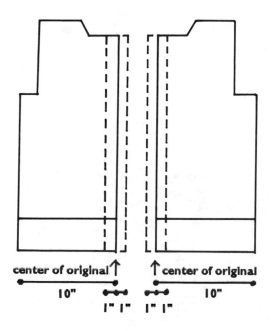

center of original ↑   ↑ center of original

10"   1" 1"   1" 1"   10"

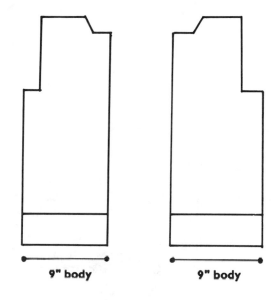

9" body   9" body

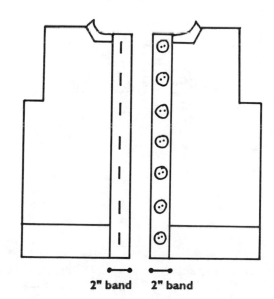

2" band   2" band

For a 40-inch-circumference crew-neck sweater, the total front width is 20 inches. For a cardigan, the front is split into two sides, each 10 inches wide. If the button and buttonhole bands are to be 2 inches wide, then they are made to extend 1 inch on either side of the center front line, giving the new fronts a 9-inch body width. In this example, the bands are knitted by picking up stitches along the fronts after the neck ribbing has been added. The decreases necessary to shape the neck were worked out on the appropriate Graph Paper.

Advanced Shape Modifications

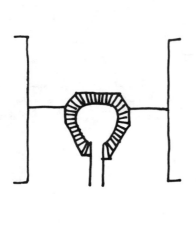

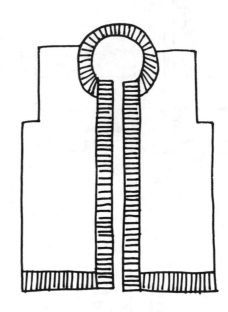

This child's crew-neck cardigan is based on the Basic Sweater using a crew-neck shaping of 5 inches wide by 4 inches deep (and extra-long ribbed sleeve bands). After the pieces were sewed together, stitches were picked up around the neck and worked in K1, P1 ribbing for 1 inch. Then stitches were picked up along the front edges from the neck to the waistband and worked in K1, P1 ribbing for 1½ inches. Buttonholes were worked evenly spaced on the buttonhole band. (See also page 54.)

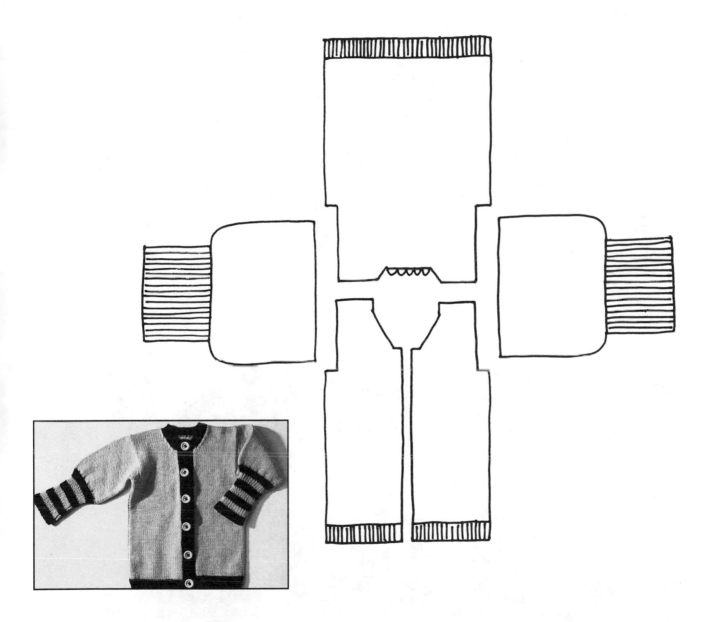

Advanced Shape Modifications

■

A V-neck cardigan

Let's suppose that we're going to knit a V-neck cardigan that is 40 inches in circumference and has 2-inch ribbed button and buttonhole bands that are knitted simultaneously with each garment front. Let's also suppose we want a 3-inch band of ribbing at the waist which will be knitted in the same K1, P1 ribbing as the button and buttonhole bands, the V-neck shaping will start at the point where the body and the yoke meet, and the body will be worked in stockinette.

Again, if the total circumference of the sweater is 40 inches, each half of the front would originally measure 10 inches. To calculate the stockinette part of the fronts, subtract the 1-inch overlap from the original body width:

10 inches − 1 inch = 9 inches

These 9 inches are worked in stockinette. To determine the total width of each front section, add the new body width to the width of the band:

9 inches + 2 inches of band = 11 inches

Each front section, then, is a total of 11 inches wide. The first 3 inches at the waist are worked in ribbing. Then 9 inches of the body width change to stockinette, and 2 inches forming the band continue in the ribbing pattern.

The V-neck shaping is plotted on Graph Paper that matches the gauge. The gauged diagram then becomes the working pattern for the yoke. Remember that the neck decreases are worked in the stockinette portion of the fronts, a few stitches in from the ribbed band.

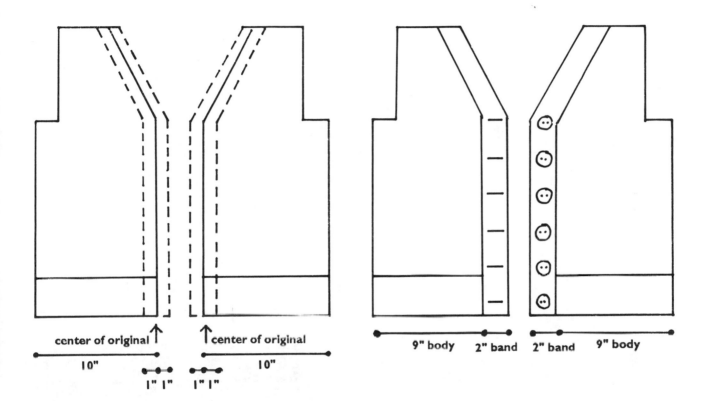

center of original ↑   ↑ center of original

10"   10"

1" 1"   1" 1"

9" body   2" band   2" band   9" body

In a 40-inch-circumference V-neck cardigan with 2-inch bands that are knitted simultaneously with the fronts, the front is split as in the crew-neck version so that the stockinette portion of each front is 9 inches wide. Adding 2-inch-wide bands to each front gives a total width of 11 inches. The decreases necessary to shape the neck can be worked out on the appropriate Graph Paper.

Advanced Shape Modifications

■

This child's short-sleeved V-neck cardigan is based on the Basic Sweater using a contracted yoke and a V-neck shaping of 5 inches wide by 7½ inches long. The 2-inch bands were worked simultaneously with the fronts. See also page 55.

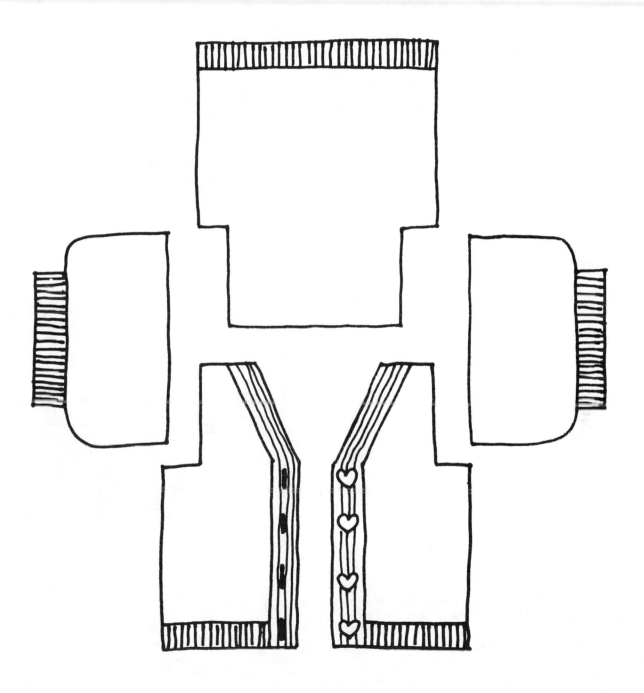

Advanced Shape Modifications
■

A double-breasted cardigan

In addition to zippered and button-up cardigans, double-breasted versions can also be made. Double-breasted sweaters don't have button and buttonhole bands; instead, each front section is extended and the two are overlapped. Buttons and buttonholes are placed on the overlapping sections. To avoid the curling which normally occurs with stockinette stitch, use a stitch such as seed stitch which will allow the pieces to lie flat. Be sure to work your gauge swatch in the same stitch.

To determine how big to make the overlap, it's helpful to use measurements that relate to other parts of the garment. For example, make the overlapped section correspond to the width of the neck opening.

To make a double-breasted sweater, form a square neck and make the amount of overlap equal to the width of the neck. Be sure to use a stitch that will keep the edges from curling—I suggest a seed stitch (K1, P1 across the first row over an even number of stitches; P1, K1 across the next; repeat). The yoke can be worked in K1, P1 ribbing for textural contrast. See also page 54.

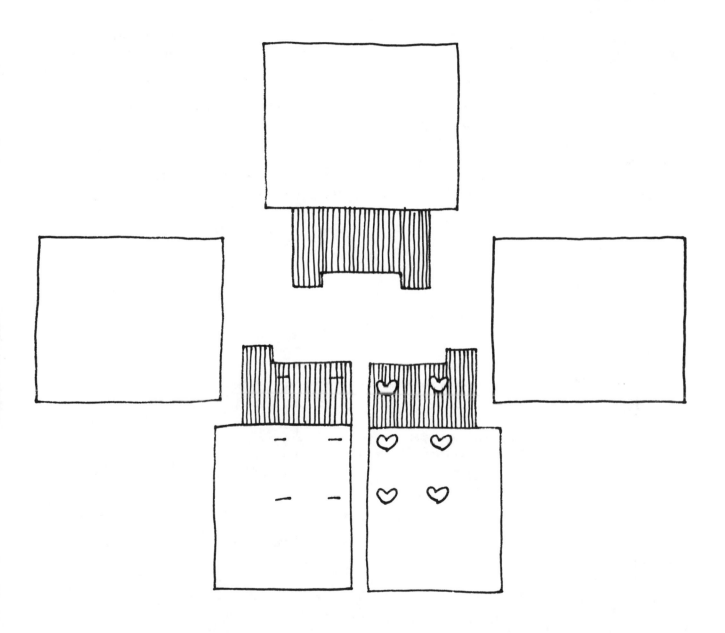

Advanced Shape Modifications

■

A word of caution

The most important thing to remember in modifying the yoke is this: **The sum of all parts must equal the total number of inches required in the yoke.** For example, in the basic adult sweater, the yoke is 16 inches × 16 inches. The saddle shoulder modification consists of 6 inches of yoke (length) in front and back, plus the 4-inch (width) saddle:

6 inches + 6 inches + 4 inches = 16 inches.

The neck opening measures 6 inches (wide) in the center, plus the two 5-inch (long) saddles on each side:

5 inches + 5 inches + 6 inches = 16 inches.

This same principle applies to all other yoke sizes (for example, the yoke in a child's sweater should measure 12 inches × 12 inches) and when designing a cardigan. Once the front section has been split into two parts, the sum of these two parts must equal the whole of the body front. In addition, if you want to include buttons, you must allow for overlapping of the two bands when calculating the number of stitches needed.

Saddle shoulder

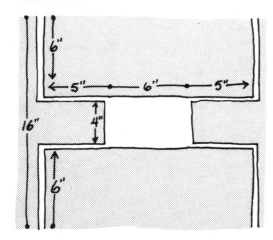

V-neck

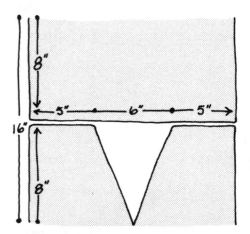

Crew neck

Crew-neck cardigan

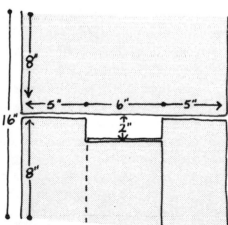

Double-breasted cardigan

In all neck variations, the sum of all of the parts must equal the total number of inches required in the yoke. No matter what the shape modification is, the dimensions of the modular yoke remain the same as shown in these variations of the adult sweater.

Putting It All Together: A Case Study

Designing children's sweaters is a joy because, on the whole, children are less critical and less inhibited than adults. One can experiment freely with color and motif, and inject a sense of fun and adventure into the design. Best of all, children's sweaters are small, so they take less time to knit!

With these things in mind, and using my granddaughter, Tiffany, as a handy model, I designed the "School Bus Sweater" shown on pages 56 and 101 as a case study in how to use the Basic Sweater pattern and Gauged Graph Paper. The school bus and schoolhouse are images that I've used often. These particular ones were taken from a work called "Here Comes the School Bus" (see page 56).

My first step was to choose the yarn, a worsted-weight wool in cream with red and yellow for the schoolhouse and bus.

I made a gauge swatch using the needle size recommended by the yarn manufacturer, and then made two more—using needles one size larger and one size smaller. I chose the gauge swatch that was 4.5 stitches to the inch and 6 rows to the inch and used the Worksheet to calculate my working pattern.

Next, I determined the shape I wanted the sweater to be. I decided that a V-neck cardigan with short sleeves would be practical and comfortable during warm autumn days. The short sleeves would would be finished with a ribbed band. The back could be worked the same as the Basic Sweater. The front, however, would take more planning. I used copies of the appropriate Gauged Graph Paper (4.5 x 6) to work out the V-neck shaping and cardigan opening.

The next step was to incorporate the schoolhouse and school bus motifs into the sweater. I drew a series of motifs directly onto copies of the Gauged Graph Paper until I was satisfied with the sizes and shapes. Because the original art work was laid out like a game board, it seemed appropriate to make the bus route continuous around the sweater yoke. In order to have the road continuous around the sleeves, I contracted the yoke so that the sleeves would be set further into the body of the sweater. I recalculated my working dimensions on the Worksheet accordingly.

I made a full-size pattern of the sweater by taping together sheets of the graph paper and drew in the bus route. I decided to place the schoolhouse in the center back. I moved my school bus motifs around until I liked the overall effect, then I taped the motifs in place. At this point, knitting the sweater was easy—I simply followed the life-size pattern plotted on my Gauged Graph paper!

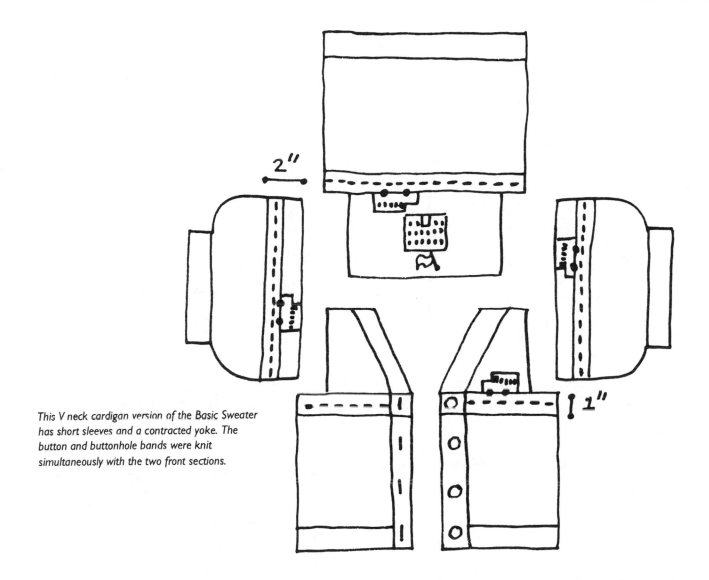

This V neck cardigan version of the Basic Sweater has short sleeves and a contracted yoke. The button and buttonhole bands were knit simultaneously with the two front sections.

I played with possible positions of the schoolhouse, school bus, and road motifs until I was satisfied. I taped together enough copies of 4.5 x 6 Gauged Graph Paper to accommodate the entire sweater and plotted the motifs and shapings directly on the paper. This then became my working pattern.

Putting It All Together

■

4.5 x 6

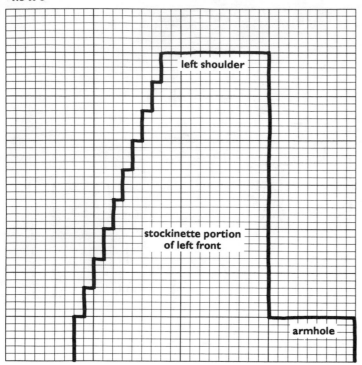

I plotted the V-neck shaping on 4.5 x 6 Graph Paper, placing the decreases on every fourth row. Though the button and buttonhole band stitches are not shown here, I decided to work 2-inch-wide (9-stitch) bands simultaneously with the sweater fronts.

4.5 x 6

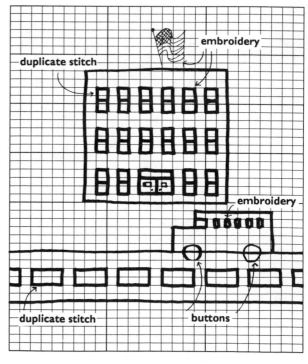

I worked out the schoolhouse, school bus, and road motifs on 4.5 x 6 Graph Paper.

Details in the schoolhouse, school bus, and road motifs were added with buttons, duplicate stitch, and embroidery.

Bibliography

■

Bibliography

The following publications contain ideas and information on motifs and/or stitch patterns that can be incorporated into a Basic Sweater design to produce additional variations.

Abbey, Barbara. *The Complete Book of Knitting.* New York: The Viking Press, 1971. Contains many stitch patterns. For hand knitters.

Bro\Brother Knitting Patterns. Book of machine-made stitch patterns. Helpful to Brother machine owners. Clever machine knitters who own different brands of machines should be able to adapt the diagrammed instructions. For machine knitters.

Chatterton, Pauline. *Scandinavian Knitting Design.* New York: Charles Scribner's Sons, 1977. Many color motifs shown charted on square paper; thus adapting the designs to your Gauged Graph Paper is an easy process. Useful to hand and machine knitters.

Duckworth, Susan. *Susan Duckworth's Knitting.* New York: Ballantine, 1988. Motifs and charted designs that can be adapted to both hand and machine versions of the Basic Sweater.

Lewis, Susanna. *A Machine Knitter's Guide to Creating Fabrics.* Asheville, NC: Lark Communications, 1986. A wealth of machine knitted fabric swatches with detailed instructions for each. Also includes graphed designs. This book is for knitters who have mastered the basics and are ready to move up to more advanced projects.

Lorant, Tessa. *Hand & Machine Knitted Laces.* London: B.T. Batsford Ltd, 1982. Traditional and modern lace patterns. Useful to both hand and machine knitters once they have mastered the basics.

Mon Tricot Knitting Dictionary: 900 Stitches and Patterns. New York: Crown, 1971. Mostly stitch patterns plus a few color motifs. For hand knitters.

Selfridge, Gail. *Patchwork Knitting.* New York: Watson-Guptill, 1977. The forerunner of the *Sweater Design Workbook* and the best existing source for additional motifs. Contains many motifs diagrammed in three gauges (4×5, 5×7, 6×8). No longer in print, but still available at many public libraries. Useful to hand and machine knitters.

The following books will provide you with ideas for modification by reshaping the parts.

Davidson, Carmen, and MaryAnn Davis. *Knitter's Guide to Sweater Design.* Loveland, Colorado: Interweave Press, 1989. A comprehensive approach to sweater styling. For hand and machine knitters.

Duncan, Ida Reilly. *Knit to Fit.* New York: Liveright, 1970. For hand and machine knitters.

_____. *The Complete Book of Progressive Knitting.* New York: Liveright, 1971. For hand and machine knitters.

Fee, Jacqueline. *The Sweater Workshop.* Loveland, Colorado: Interweave Press, 1983. A method for knitting raglan-sleeved sweaters in a variety of styles. For hand knitters.

Passap abc. Available through Passap knitting machine dealers. Deals with shaping parts of sweaters. Machine knitters only.

Thomas, Mary. *Mary Thomas's Knitting Book.* New York: Dover, 1972. For hand and machine knitters.

In addition to hand knitting and machine knitting, the Basic Sweater can also be executed in crochet. Here are some sources of ideas for making a crocheted version.

Feldman, Dell Pitt. *Crochet Discovery and Design.* New York: Doubleday & Co., Inc., 1972.

Sommer, Elyse and Mike. *A New Look at Crochet* New York: Crown Publishers, Inc., 1975.

Care and Use of the Masters

The master Worksheet, Planning Guide, and Gauged Graph Papers are on the following pages. *Never* write directly on them. Instead, work on photocopies of the masters.

Use the Worksheet to calculate your working pattern from your gauge and body measurements. Use the Planning Guide to work out motif possibilities. Use the Gauged Graph Papers to plot your motifs at the same proportion that they will be knitted.

Once your gauge is established, check the Gauged Graph Papers to find one that comes the closest to matching your gauge. In most cases, one of the Graph Papers will match your gauge exactly, but in the event that there is not one that matches your gauge, you have two options.

1. If it's a matter of a slight difference, knit a new swatch, making it either tighter or looser, until it corresponds to the gauge of one of the papers.

2. Pick the paper that most closely approximates your gauge, disregard the inch markings, and simply designate the required number of stitches and rows represented by your gauge.

For example, suppose your gauge is 6 stitches per inch and 9 rows per inch and you want to diagram a 4-inch-square area. Though there is no 6 × 9 gauged paper, you can modify the 6 × 8 paper. The 6 stitch divisions per inch would remain the same, but there would be 36, and not 32, rows in 4 inches. You can simply draw a line at the 36-row mark and work your motif in this area. While the resulting diagram is slightly distorted, it is much more in proportion than if you had used squared paper.

3. You can also modify the papers. For example, if your gauge has twice the stitches and rows per inch as one of the Gauged Graph Papers, you can simply use a ruler and divide each square in half both vertically and horizontally.

For more gauge possibilities (more than 200 papers), look for Gail Selfridge's Graph-It!, *available from Interweave Press.*

WORKSHEET: making a working pattern

Record your measurements on this worksheet. Then use your gauge information to convert inches of the pattern to numbers of stitches and number of rows.

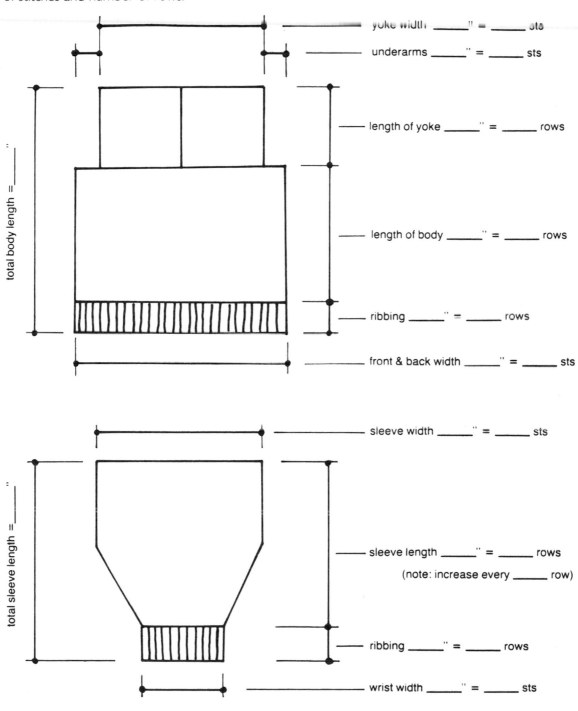

yoke width _____" = _____ sts

underarms _____" = _____ sts

length of yoke _____" = _____ rows

length of body _____" = _____ rows

ribbing _____" = _____ rows

front & back width _____" = _____ sts

sleeve width _____" = _____ sts

sleeve length _____" = _____ rows

(note: increase every _____ row)

ribbing _____" = _____ rows

wrist width _____" = _____ sts

total body length = _____

total sleeve length = _____

YARN & MACHINE NOTES:

hem notes (optional) _____" = _____ rows

PLANNING GUIDE. This is the master Planning Guide. All work is done on copies of the master.

5 x 5

4 x 5

4.5 x 5

5 x 6

5 x 6

x 7

5 x 8

5 x 7

5.5 x 8

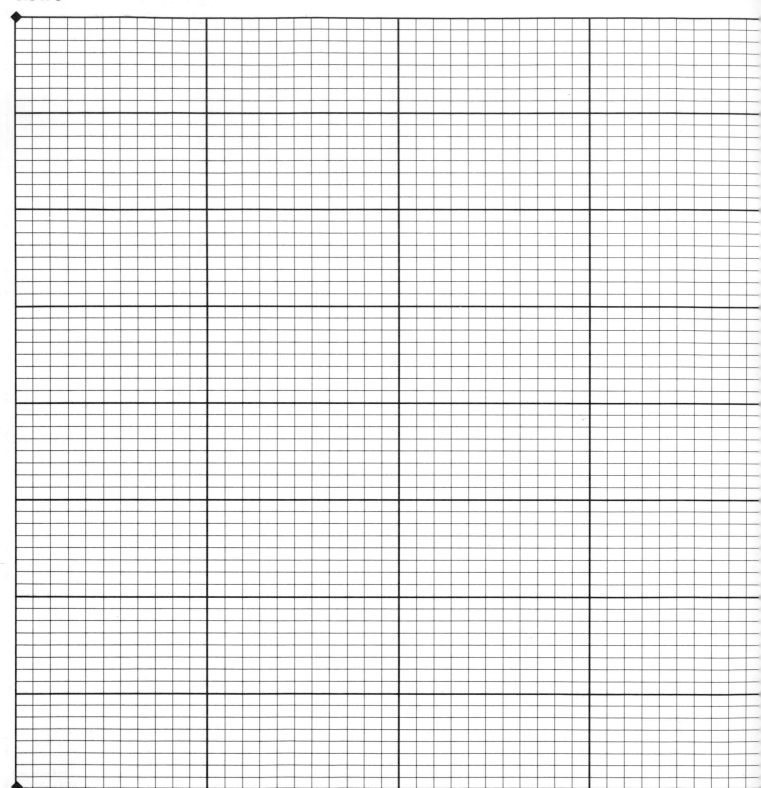

6 x 8

5 x 8

7 x 9

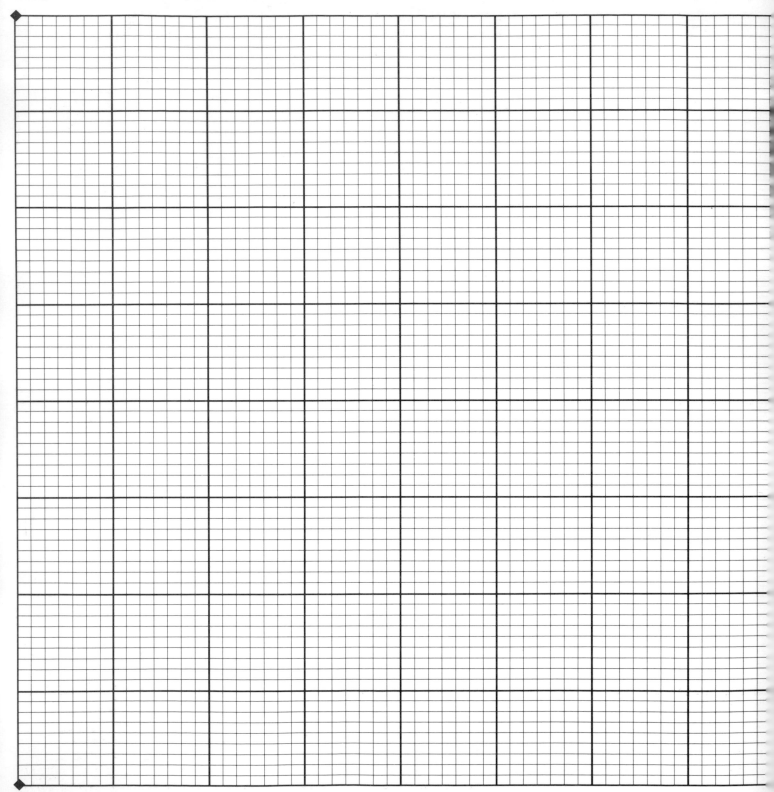

7.5 x 10

8.5 x 11

9.5 x 11